INSOMNIAC DREAMS

EXPERIMENTS WITH TIME BY

Vladimir Nabokov

COMPILED, EDITED, & WITH COMMENTARIES BY
GENNADY BARABTARLO

PRINCETON UNIVERSITY PRESS
Princeton & Oxford

Compilation, preface, parts 1 and 5, notes, and other editorial material copyright © 2018 by Princeton University Press

Requests for permission to reproduce material from this work should be sent to Permissions, Princeton University Press

PUBLISHED BY PRINCETON UNIVERSITY PRESS
41 William Street, Princeton, New Jersey 08540

IN THE UNITED KINGDOM: PRINCETON UNIVERSITY PRESS
6 Oxford Street, Woodstock, Oxfordshire OX20 1TR

press.princeton.edu

Jacket images courtesy of Alamy
Jacket design by Chris Ferrante

Owing to limitations of space, all acknowledgments for permission to reprint previously published material can be found on page 191

FRONTISPIECE: Vladimir Nabokov writing in bed at home in Ithaca, New York, 1958. (Photo by Carl Mydans / Time Life Pictures / Getty Images)

All images in this book except the frontispiece are from the Berg Collection of English and American Literature, The New York Public Library, Astor, Lenox and Tilden Foundations. Copyright © the Dmitri Nabokov Estate. Used by permission of The Wylie Agency, LLC.

ISBN 978-0-691-16794-7

Library of Congress Control Number: 2017941575

British Library Cataloging-in-Publication Data is available

This book has been composed in Baskerville 10 Pro

Printed on acid-free paper. ∞

PRINTED IN THE UNITED STATES OF AMERICA

10 9 8 7 6 5 4 3 2 1

IN MEMORIAM DMITRI NABOKOV

What is Time? If no one asks me, I know;
if I wish to explain it to one that asketh, I know not.

—St. Augustine, *The Confessions*, Book XI

CONTENTS

ILLUSTRATIONS

PREFACE

THIS BOOK WAS BORN of the convergence of two initially separate undertakings: a paper entitled "Clarity of Vision," delivered at a Nabokov conference in Auckland, New Zealand, and my studies of Nabokov's records of his 1964 experiment with dreams, as well as his diaries, preserved in the New York Public Library. The latter setting, with its sterile, hushed chill soothed by the warmth of the helpful staff, could not be more different from the playhouse of a large university auditorium.

The conference was called "Nabokov Upside Down," and my paper was read on the last day, which happened to fall on the last day of 2011 (O.S.). I have long noticed that discussing Nabokov in public often sets even experts somewhat ill at ease, with the result that almost every paper read at conferences contains, and transmits to auditors, larger than standard doses of crafted humor, summoned as if to cover the uneasiness that this uncomfortable genius causes in a contemporary mind. My text, however, was straight-faced humorless. Its subject was, as is stated elsewhere in this book, a "staggering chance meeting an improbable alternative to chance." The conference took place in a modern, highly efficient building where, in order to save energy, rooms would go dark after a preset period of inactivity within; flail your arms, and the light might come on. This was the metaphor that at the last minute I had prepared to deploy if asked what I made of my observations, hoping that it would not be taken for a wisecrack. But I read next to last, there was little time for questions, and nobody raised a hand.

The book consists of five parts. The first sets forth the chief psycho-philosophical problem of the function and direction of memory in dreamland; introduces John Dunne's treatise on the subject of "serial Time," comparing it with the contemporary, although then largely unpublished, research by Pavel Florensky; and describes Nabokov's dream experiment, which was based on the premise and instructions gleaned in Dunne's book. The second part contains an annotated transcription of Nabokov's dreams (as well as a number of his wife's) in the fall of 1964, published for the first time,[1] which he recorded following precise instructions as set in Dunne's *Experiment with Time*. Part 3 adduces descriptions of dreams from Nabokov's American and Swiss diaries and letters, both before the 1964 experiment and after, which allows me to extend the observations and conclusions derived from the experiment (inconclusive as they are) to Nabokov's more general sleeping and specific dreaming experience and its place in his fiction. To this end, part 4 collects various fabricated dreams one encounters in Nabokov's books, both Russian and English, grouped under the categories that he defines in his experiment, with the addition of new rubrics as required: Nabokov's characters appear to have a broader range of dream variety than did their maker. The last part defines and enlarges on the subject of Nabokov's view of time as a primary structuring condition of existence and specifically of the intricate cooperation of memory and imagination in life and in fiction writing, with often an unpredictable outcome: precognitive verging on prophetic.

1. A small selection appeared, with my introduction and brief commentaries, in the *Times Literary Supplement* (October 31, 2014).

Special thanks are offered to Dr. Isaac Gewirtz, curator of the Berg Collection of the New York Public Library, and librarians Mr. Joshua McKeon and Miss Lyndsi Barnes, for their skilled and obliging assistance in my research; to Mr. Andrew Wylie and Miss Kristina Moore, of the Wylie Agency representing the Nabokov Estate, for permitting me to publish my findings; and to the Research Council of the University of Missouri, for a grant that supported some of the associated travels. I would be wanting in courtesy if I did not expressly say that I am grateful to Professor Brian Boyd who suggested an idea that went into the third part of the book, and I cannot deny myself the pleasure of publicly thanking my wife for her excellent advice to compile what was to become part 4, without which the book would have been so much leaner in substance and plot.

Forty years ago Nabokov registered his gratitude to Princeton University Press that, upon acquiring the Bollingen Series, brought out a much revised edition of his monumental translation and interpretation of *Eugene Onegin*. I, too, am indebted to the generosity of that excellent press for consenting to publish this slim book and to Miss Anne Savarese, executive editor of literature, for her unfailing enthusiasm, a large number of suggested improvements, and proficient management of the entire multitiered process that has made this book a material reality. I am thankful to Dr. Daniel Simon for his lint-roller thorough copyediting of my text; to Mr. Christopher Ferrante, whose artistic taste and skill turned it into a handsome thing; to Dr. Kathleen Cioffi, Senior Production Editor, for her imperturbable attention to smallest details and textual crotchets; and to my daughter Maria Sapp, who caught a number of important flaws at page-proof stage.

I want to make special and uncommon mention of the reader whom the press engaged to review this book for them and who went far beyond the usual reference duty and combed my text with utmost attention, so that

> no levell'd malice
> Infects one comma in the course I hold.

I owe this anonymous colleague more than I can express.

Gennady Barabtarlo

INSOMNIAC DREAMS

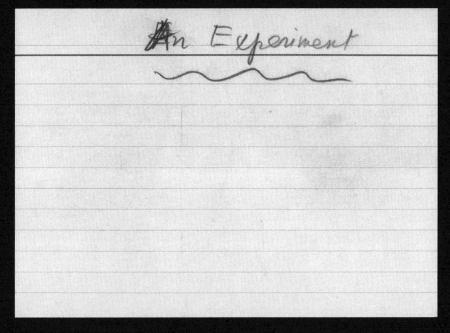

FIGURE 1. The title card for the dream-recording experiment Nabokov began in October 1964.

PART 1

CHRONIC CONDITION

DREAM, MEMORY

Time is . . . —but this book is about that.

—J. W. Dunne, *An Experiment with Time*

ON OCTOBER 14, 1964, in a grand Swiss hotel in Montreux where he had been living for three years, Vladimir Nabokov started a private experiment that lasted till January 3 of the following year, just before his wife's birthday (he had engaged her to join him in the experiment and they compared notes). Every morning, immediately upon awakening, he would write down what he could rescue of his dreams. During the following day or two he was on the lookout for anything that seemed to do with the recorded dream. One hundred and eighteen handwritten Oxford cards, now held in the Berg Collection of the New York Public Library, bear sixty-four such records, many with relevant daytime episodes.

The point of that experiment was to test a theory according to which dreams can be precognitive as well as related to the past. That theory is based on the premise that images and situations in our dreams are not merely kaleidoscoping shards, jumbled, and mislabeled fragments of past impressions, but may also be a proleptic view of an event to come—which offers, as a pleasant side bonus, a satisfactory explanation of the well-known *déjà vu* phenomenon. Dreams may also be a fanciful convolution of both past and future events. This is possible because, according to this proposition, time's progress is not unidirectional but recursive: the reason we do not notice the backflow is that we are not paying attention. Dreamland is the best proving ground.

Thirteen years prior, on January 25, 1951, Nabokov had a heart-tweaking dream about his father at the piano in their old St. Petersburg home, playing some notes of a Mozart sonata with one hand, looking sad and baffled at his son's attempted literary joke: Turgenev calls, somewhere, a forty-five-year-old man an old man, whereas he, Vladimir Nabokov, is already fifty-two. On waking up and recording it, Nabokov inserts "almost" before "fifty-two," then writes that his father was killed when he was fifty-two as well. The coincidence is indeed astounding: when Nabokov had that dream, he was *exactly* the same age as his father was on the day of his death, give or take two days.

Next he outlines a plan for what appears to be a sequel to his book of memoirs that was soon to be published.

This is another thing I ought to write, with especial stress on the sloppy production—any old backdrop will do etc.—of dreams.

1. The Three Tenses
2. Dreams
3. The one about the central European professor looking for a job.

The first item—a hull of a short story about one man's present, past, and future love affairs—he sketched in the same notebook the day before. The third item was to become his third American novel, *Pnin*: this is its first heartbeat. The item in between reflects his enduring desire to prepare his dream visions for publication, a project never realized as such, even though versions of his dreams appear in many of his writings (collected in part 4).

On February 14, 1951, his memoir *Conclusive Evidence* (of his "having existed," as he explains in the preface to the definitive 1966 edition, retitled *Speak, Memory*) is published. Four days later, he makes notes for a prospective sequel, now boldly letting the cooperative work of memory and imagination share the table of contents:

> I see quite clearly now another book, "More Evidence"—something like that—"American Part"[1]
>
> 1. Criticism and addenda of "Conclusive Evidence"
> 2. Three Tenses
> 3. Dreams
> 4. MCZ and collecting (merge back into Russia)[2]
> 5. St Mark's (with full details)[3]
> 6. Story I am doing now[4]
> 7. Double Talk (enlarged)[5]
> 8. Edmund W.[6]

1. Nabokov wrote parts for a sequel book tentatively entitled *Speak On, Memory*, about his life in America, but never completed it.

2. In the 1940s Nabokov worked at Harvard's Museum of Comparative Zoology as a curator of their lepidoptera collections.

3. Nabokov's son, Dmitri, went to St. Mark's, a prep school in Southborough, Massachusetts; it served as a model for "St Bartholomew's" school in *Pnin* (1957). In her notes of 1958, Véra Nabokov recalled that the school was "very disappointing, inferior teachers, headmaster vulgar cad, good adjustment [at Dexter, Dmitri's previous school] destroyed by unfair ludicrous treatment" (Berg Collection of the New York Public Library).

4. "The Vane Sisters," an episode for which ("Exam") was set down in this notebook on January 26, with an addition jotted on facing page eight years later, when Nabokov was revising the story for publication.

5. A 1945 short story, later retitled (but not enlarged) "Conversation Piece, 1945."

6. The writer and critic Edmund Wilson, who at the time was Nabokov's good friend.

February 18

I see quite clearly now another book
"More Evidence" — something like that —
"American" part

1   Criticism and addenda of "Conclusive Evidence"
2.   Three Tenses
3.   Dreams
4.   MCZ and collecting (merge back into Russia
5   St Mark's (with full details)
6   Story I am doing now
7   Double Talk (enlarged)
8   Edmund W.
9   The assistant professor who was never found out
10   (Cross, Fairbanks)
11
12
13
14
15   Criticism and addenda to this "

9. *The assistant professor* who was *never* found out
(Cross, Fairbanks)[7]

10.

11.

12.

13.

14.

15. Criticism and addenda to this.

It is very likely that Nabokov meant to mold his later dream experiment into a literary form as well, perhaps with a view to incorporating excerpts into his second book of autobiography.

DUNNE AND HIS THEORY

1.

The hypothesis behind Nabokov's experiment was advanced by John W. Dunne, a pioneering early twentieth-century British aeronautical engineer, eccentric writer, and original thinker. Between 1901 and 1914 Dunne invented and constructed a "heavier-than-air" flying apparatus for military reconnaissance, which went through ten iterations, both mono- and biplanes, from the D.[unne]1 to D.10. It had an arrowhead body, with wings swept back as in the modern delta designs, and had no tail, which, paradoxically, lent the plane

7. Nabokov was highly critical of the way the Russian language was taught in America in general and at Cornell in particular; one can catch reflection of this dissatisfaction in *Pnin*. Professor Samuel Hazzard Cross (1891–1946) was a Slavic scholar at Harvard, "who knows only the middle of Russian words and completely ignores prefixes and endings" (VN's letter to Roman Grynberg of December 25, 1943; see Boyd-1991, 69). Associate professor Gordon H. Fairbanks, whose grasp of the language was even weaker, was nevertheless in charge of Russian-language instruction at Cornell, much to Nabokov's chagrin (Boyd-1991, 196–97).

an amazing stability. Dunne could control it by applying throttle alone by foot, his hands free to take notes in flight.

The trends in aircraft construction before World War I were veering sharply away from his design, and, beset by congenital heart illness, Dunne abandoned aviation. After a period spent devising new and improved ways of dry-fly fishing (Dunne published, in 1924, an influential book on the subject of making artificial flies "translucent," the way fish would see the real flies through sunlight), he turned to research that would allow him to explain to his satisfaction a strange series of dreams that he had had since his youth and that, as he discovered, others had experienced, too. He studied contemporary theories of Time, from C. H. Hinton's *What Is the Fourth Dimension?* (1887) to Bergson and Freud, on one hand, and to Planck and Einstein, on the other. Encouraged by H. G. Wells, an old friend of his, he came up with a detailed general theory, which he published in 1927 as *An Experiment with Time* (by a curious coincidence, the same year that Heidegger published *Sein und Zeit,* perhaps his most profound work). Dunne's book has gone through numerous editions, the best being the revised third, published in 1934 with numerous reprints, of which Nabokov owned one. The book caused considerable stir in scholarly philosophical circles and had an ideological influence on a number of contemporary anglophone writers, notably Aldous Huxley and J. B. Priestley, and perhaps less obviously on James Joyce, Walter de la Mare, and T. S. Eliot.[8]

Dunne developed and honed his theory of serial Time in several later books, some with titles that could have caught

8. A curious passage in Eugene Jolas's memoirs refers to Dunne. Jolas writes that he read to Joyce, in Paris, after one of Joyce's eye surgeries, the "brilliant *Experiment with Time* which Joyce regarded highly." Jolas goes on to relate two remarkable dreams that Joyce remembered, the first of which confirms Dunne's proposition much too literally to be above the suspicion of a leg-pull. See Eugene Jolas, *Man from Babel*, 167.

Nabokov's attention, although there is no evidence that Nabokov read them: *The New Immortality* (1938) and especially *Nothing Dies*, published in 1940, the year Nabokov with his wife and son migrated to America from Europe, in which violent death became as ordinary and predictable as foul weather.[9]

2.

Dunne's *Experiment with Time* is peculiar on all sides. It is utterly original in premise, composition, and style, the latter owing in part to the fact that the author is not a professional *literatus* bound by conventions. He puts the practical application of his hypothesis before the hypothesis. He sprinkles his narration with rhetorical questions of the type "Can we now be certain that [yclept] be true?", and answers them with an immediate and firm "Yes, we can," dispensing even with customary qualifiers. He uses italics with annoying frequency, as if always suspecting that the reader's attention is flagging and every now and then tugging at his sleeve (". . . the argument is *based* upon the hypothesis . . ."; ". . . a three-dimensional *observer* . . ."). He dismisses competitive theories for which he has no use—that is, almost all of them. Nevertheless, his slim book makes for fascinating reading.

The introduction is doubtless one of the most idiosyncratic ever written. "The general reader will find the book demands from him no previous knowledge of science, mathematics, philosophy, or psychology," Dunne writes. "It is considerably easier to understand than are, say, the rules of Contract Bridge. The exception is the remainder of this Introduction." The real exception for this reader, however, is the second,

9. That book led Borges to write a remarkably concise and lucid summary of Dunne's theory of infinite regression and its origins, "Time and J. W. Dunne" (1940). See Jorge Luis Borges, *Selected Non-Fictions*, 217–19.

theoretical, part of the book filled with baffling figures, some distinguishable only by an addition of an arrow point to what was just a line in the previous diagram.

Dunne straddles a curiously uncomfortable ridge, clear of both physics and metaphysics. Of the former he says, shrewdly: "Physics is . . . a science which has been expressly designed to study, not the universe, but the things which would supposedly remain in that universe if we were to abstract therefrom every effect of a purely sensory character." In other words, physical science principally ignores the subjective observer, the word Dunne likes to emphasize.[10] Physics is not interested in sensory perceptions, including the *sense* of time. The observer must be removed, for he is "a permanent obstacle in the path of our search for external reality." For Dunne, the human observer is a cardinal element of the entire system.

On the other hand, Dunne states in the introduction that his theory is decidedly free of mysticism, clairvoyance, or prophecy, that it is not "a book about 'occultism' and not a book about what is called 'psycho-analysis,'" after which he nonchalantly announces that "incidentally, it contains the first scientific argument for human immortality. This, I may say, was entirely unexpected." Forsooth.

This philosophical ambiguity informs the entire exposition, which does not seem to trouble Dunne in the least. He presents a long string of dreams, astonishing in their exact precognition of a subsequent event or situation, then proceeds to show, in mathematical terms, that this wonder is universal and perfectly logical. There is a dreamlike quality to his explanations. He admits that "the incidents in question mimicked to perfection many classical examples of 'clairvoyance,'

10. In any event, it ignored the observer at the time of Dunne's writing, for in later years physical science has had to reckon with the act of observation interfering with what is being observed, as in quantum demolition measurements.

'astral-wandering,' and 'messages from the dead'" (his mention of the latter must have caught Nabokov's eye, since a much subtler version of the spiritual interference was the subject of many of Nabokov's metaphysical plots.)[11] Early on, Dunne proposes that "the idea of a soul must have first arisen in the mind of primitive man as the result of observation of his dreams. Ignorant as he was, he could have come to no other conclusion but that, in dreams, he left his sleeping body in one universe and went wandering off into another."

It is not unreasonable to assume that Nabokov turned the pages of the book's second, theoretical, part faster. The chapters that follow the dream puzzles and the experiment précis are written in a quaint, hard-boiled yet lively, even blithe, diction, but what started as a promisingly great detective story now turns into a complex of applied algebraic formulas that use up much of the Latin alphabet and are illustrated by drab diagrams. Here is a good example—a sentence Proustian in length, Carollian in its calm desultoriness:

> If, then, $G'G''$ represents that state of the cerebrum where it first (in Time I) becomes sufficiently developed to allow the ultimate observer to perceive psychological effects, and if $H'H''$ represents the place where (in Time I) that cerebrum ceases its useful activity and disintegrates, we may say that observer 2 can observe the *whole* of his ordinary, waking, Time I life, from birth to death, but that, for some reason to be determined, he allows his *attention* to follow observer 1 in that individual's journey from left to right (from birth to death) along field 2.

Even an earnest reader might feel, halfway through this serpentine sentence, that his "cerebrum ceases its useful activity and disintegrates"—a marked difference from the previous

---

11. See Boyd-1991, Alexandrov-1993, Barabtarlo-1993 and 2011.

mode of narration, especially the brisk and engaging description of his strange dreams.

3.

Dunne recounts that his first unusual dream of the series took place at a Sussex hotel at 3:30 a.m. in 1899. It is hard to imagine that Nabokov, born that year, could hold back a smile at the coincidence when he read that. That first dream, notably, had to do with time: Dunne dreamed that his watch had stopped, then awoke to discover that his watch lying on the chest of drawers had stopped at precisely the same time, to the minute, as the watch in his dream. The second episode took place in Sorrento, when in a semiwaking state he saw a mental projection of the clock face that he could not see physically, showing the exact time. There is a curious analogy to both of these episodes in Nabokov's 1937 short story "Cloud, Castle, Lake," in which the main character "slept badly the night before the departure. And why? Because he had to get up unusually early, and hence took along into his dreams the delicate face of the watch ticking on his night table" (*Stories*, 430).

Three ever more striking and inexplicable incidents of precognitive dreaming followed, causing Dunne to suspect that his case was what was known as *identifying paramnesia:* unwittingly making up a preceding dream to match a later waking experience. Starting with the fifth, in 1904—in which he saw a devastating fire of a building in singular detail, then read, in the evening paper, a report of a big fire at a rubber factory near Paris with an uncanny number of the same dreadful details as in his dream—he began to set down such dreams right upon awakening, which was to become the chief requirement of his experiment, to make certain that no "identifying paramnesia" was at work.

Dunne's sixth perplexing dream occurred also in 1904, in an Austrian hotel with the curious name *Scholastika*. (It may be worth noting that most of these dreams happened while the dreamer was sleeping in hotel beds; during *his* experiment, and for the rest of his life, Nabokov held residence in Montreux Palace hotel.) At that point Dunne realized that these dreams would have "exhibited nothing in the smallest degree unusual" had they happened on the nights *"after the corresponding events,"* but they occurred on the *"wrong,"* i.e., preceding, nights (all italics are Dunne's). Thus he understands that the events he sees in the dreamland are displaced in time.

The seventh installment had to do with a 1912 monoplane crash in which his friend perished near Oxford: at the same time that very morning, in Paris, Dunne saw that very man wrecking his plane in a field but walking away from the crash. He thought that this new striking evidence could be, if one were so inclined, taken for a message from the "spirit-world" or a "phantasm of the dying"; the quotation marks are Dunne's, to signify that he himself did not believe in any of these concepts—unlike Nabokov, who did, and who likely ticked the phrases in the margins of his copy.

The last item Dunne records occurred in the autumn of 1913, when he saw in a dream a train wreck, again in precise detail. Half a year later, on April 14, 1914, the mail train *Flying Scotsman* jumped the parapet.

The descriptions of the dreams are meticulous, methodical, level-headed; they appear reliable, although unexplained oddities crop up here and there. It is unclear, for instance, why all eight dreams reported in the book were "carefully memorized" and not written down at once. Instead of the exact dates on which they occurred, Dunne usually gives seasons or just the year, which stands in strange disagreement with the general precision of the presentation.

Dunne realized very early on that he might be able to discover some entirely new aspect of the structure of Time. The dreams themselves were not out of the ordinary, but he saw that "large blocks of otherwise perfectly normal personal experience [were] displaced from their proper positions in Time."

4.

The experiment proper is laid out methodically in part 3 of Dunne's book. He was looking for evidence that his predictive dreams were neither abnormal nor peculiar to him alone, but pointed to the previously overlooked aspect of Time and thus must be common to all. People, he noted, tend to forget their dreams upon awakening or else "fail to notice the connection with the subsequent, related event." Occasionally snatches of old dreams surface: there may lurk a plausible explanation of what is known as a *déjà vu,* a sequence of events seen in a dream but utterly forgotten until the event happens in waking life, sometimes years later.

Dunne therefore concludes that dreams generally are composed of "images of past experience and images of future experience blended together in approximately equal proportions." His prime argument is that the world is stretched out in time but we have a curiously distorted notion of it, "a view with the 'future' part unaccountably missing, cut off from the growing 'past' part by a travelling 'present moment,'" a habitual fallacy owing to a "purely mentally imposed barrier which existed only when we were awake."

It was at that point that Dunne devised his singular experiment in order to test whether what he himself experienced was not idiosyncratic but common to all. He engaged three other persons to try it, following his meticulous instructions—with spectacular results, some better than his own.

He developed the technical side with a view to overcoming two chief impediments that do not let us track time in more than one direction: the difficulty of retaining the memory of a dream and the greater difficulty of relating it to a subsequent event, of making plausible the connection between the events presented themselves in the dream world and in the waking world. Most people remember some of their dreams, a good number have recorded some of them, yet "not one in a thousand through all the past centuries seems to have *noticed* that he dreams of the future" (italics are Dunne's, of course).

Nabokov must have read the instructions with attention because he seems to have followed most of them carefully, at least at the beginning of his experiment. They are, says Dunne, "one and all, of extreme importance. Indeed, it may be safely said that, unless the reader follows them in every detail, he will be reducing his chances of getting results almost to vanishing point." In the third edition Dunne added several pages of clarifications and additional instructions, after having received confused reports from the readers of the first two editions.

5.

To a pre-twentieth-century consciousness, the phenomenon Dunne describes would seem flatly opposed to the conventional view of time legislated by the unassailable structure of physics. "In these circumstances, our hypothetical dreamer would have had to take refuge in Mysticism. He would have had to accept the existence of two disconnected worlds, the one rational, the other irrational," says Dunne. But what if the two worlds are not disconnected? Deep inside, Nabokov was a mystic after a fashion, and the notion of metaphysical interfusion with, even intervention into, one's life was very close to him, a translucent backdrop in most of his fiction.

Neither Nabokov nor Dunne was aware of an extraordinary study undertaken at the time of Dunne's experiment, both parallel and contrastive to Dunne's proposition: Pavel Florensky's *Iconostasis* (1919–22, first published posthumously, as were most of his works).[12] Florensky (1882–1937), a Russian priest, profound theologian, and philosopher of genius,[13] begins his now-famous essay on the theology of the icon by considering time dynamics in dreams. Florensky's departure point is the same as Dunne's: dreams occur in the realm that may hold the key to the fundamental truth about the world we inhabit and its chief structural condition and dimension, Time. He lists classical experiments with dreams, but his premise and conclusions are different: "The Creed names God 'the Creator of things visible and invisible.' [. . .] The two worlds—visible and invisible—are contagious. However, their difference is so great that the question of the *border* of their contact arises inevitably. It divides them whilst also uniting them."[14]

Both Dunne and Florensky employed mathematical methods to reckon the mystery of timeflow in dreams and describe the puzzle of proleptic dreaming; in contrast to modern physicists, both understood the central importance to physical science of a human observer's perception and psychology. The deep philosophical difference between the two is that while Dunne attempts to explain the baffling phenomenon within the constraints of natural science, Florensky's thought

12. My rendition of that part of Florensky's tract follows closely the definitive Russian edition (Florensky-1996, vol. 2, 419–526). An imperfect English translation by D. Sheehan and Olga Andrejev was published in 1996: Pavel Florensky, *Iconostasis*.

13. There is a recent English biography of Florensky by Avril Pyman, *Pavel Florensky: A Quiet Genius. The Tragic and Extraordinary Life of Russia's Unknown da Vinci* (2010). The subtitle is curiously inappropriate since Florensky's worldview stood in principal opposition to what is known as Renaissance culture in general and to Leonardo da Vinci especially.

14. Florensky-1996, 419, my translation.

transcends the limits of science and probes metaphysical possibilities. A world inaccessible to our five senses is not merely real—more real perhaps than the one sensually perceived—but the two worlds are contiguous, even imbricated, and dreams are the twilight zone of their overlap.

Dunne's working hypothesis is that Time should be perceived as a series of new dimensions, or layers, ever unfolding before the mind of an observer into a receding mental vista: time that *times* the passage of Time, measures it to infinity. The system resembles the Chinese-boxes principle: every "time" is contained in a larger time that times its progress. The old notion of Time serving as a fourth dimension of the universe, which Einstein and other relativists developed into a theory of pliable space-time, receives here what Dunne calls "a sensory centre" of observation, and the number of dimensions multiplies aoristically—a direction that physical and mathematical thought took up for study much later. His dream theory is situated somewhere between two extreme contemporary positions: it dismisses Freud's proposition—with a shrug rather than the scorn that Nabokov held for it—that dreams are a reflection of one's base self, stirring up unconscious motions and images; yet it does not reach into the spiritual realm of Florensky's view that dreams are the zone of contact of the two worlds. For Dunne, dreams present reasonable evidence of time's regression. His rational consciousness argument thus sits neatly above Freud's subconscious and Florensky's superconscious one, both nonrational at their diametrically opposite planes, each contrary to Dunne's stance in its own way. What is a contradiction to Dunne is an antinomy for Florensky: one is a "wrong way" sign while the other is a warning to proceed with great caution, if at all.

"Dream is the first and simplest—in the sense of our being completely accustomed to it—stage of the life in the invisible [world]," says Florensky. "Allowing that this stage is the lowest one, at least it is most often the lowest, dream, even in its coarse condition, even unschooled, exalts the soul into the invisible and grants even to the least sensitive of us a foretaste of something that differs from what we tend to consider life. We know that on the threshold of dreaming and wakefulness, as we pass the interim area—the border of their contact—our soul becomes surrounded by dreams" (419). De la Mare, one of the young Nabokov's favorite English poets, was well aware of Dunne's work and almost certainly unaware of Florensky's very existence, yet he echoes the latter rather than the former when he calls the dream zone "the borderland."[15]

It is generally accepted that vivid dream images occur during that momentary passage from one realm into the other, verifiably just before waking. The transition is timeless, or vanishingly short, but when we emerge on the other side, we install our memory of the dream in the temporal condition of our sensory world, adjusting it to fit the familiar timeflow. Nabokov, as a lifelong sufferer of severe insomnia that grew progressively worse toward the end of his life, must have been in that time zone of the so-called "rapid eye movement" longer than most, and his dreams could be more protracted and vivid and memorable. Here is Florensky's startling observation, in a compact paraphrase.

We all know that in a short dream one can live for hours, months, even years: a dreamer acquires a different means of sensing time. Above and beyond the principle of time relativity, postulating that time may pass with different speed in different closed systems (a phenomenon Nabokov detected in *Anna Karenin* and described both in his Cornell lectures

15. Walter de la Mare, *Behold, This Dreamer!*, 5–6.

and in *Pnin*), there is a theory that it may pass with an *infinite* speed, as it were turning itself inside-out like a sock, at which point it may acquire an *inverted* sense of its flow. In other words, this is Time directed from the future to the past, from effects to causes.

Sometimes a detectable outside disturbance wakes us from a dream, yet few pay attention to the *composition* of the dream's plot that the waking cause set in motion. A dream concludes on an event x, which occurred because of an earlier event t, which happened because still earlier an event s took place, caused by an r, etc. The dreamer recognizes the etiology as plausible, and it can be thus retraced all the way to the event *alpha,* perhaps insignificant by itself but one that started the entire chain. But we know that the actual cause for the whole dream was an event of circumstance (sound, smell, dropped blanket) external to the closed system of the dreamer. Florensky designates this "waking call" event by an omega. This omega causes both the dream and the alarm that arouses one from that dream. Thus x is a translation of the external cause "omega" into the depictive language of the dream world.

But the event alpha that had set off the etiological linkage within the dream has nothing to do with the omega! In other words, if at the end of a dream we see a patch of fragrant flowers (final event x) while someone in the daytime world puts a cotton ball touched with perfume to our nose (omega), then how can we explain a string of events started with the initial cause alpha that has led us to that patch? That alpha was not in any way caused by the omega. And yet without that alpha there would have been no x, that is, no dream at all, that is, we would not have been awakened by the external cause omega.

Florensky then gives a few classical examples, of which two have particular relevance to Dunne's experiment with

Time. In one, the dreamer goes on an outing in the country and comes to the neighboring village. The villagers go to church, holding their hymnals. It's a Sunday, and a service is about to begin. He wants to go there, too, but at first he takes a short rest in the churchyard. Reading inscriptions on tombstones, he takes note of the bell-ringer, who climbs to the belfry. The dreamer sees a small bell about to ring at the beginning of the mass. Soon it starts swaying, and he can hear its loud, piercing chimes, so loud, in fact, that he wakes up. The alarm clock is the cause.[16]

A much more elaborate example of the cause-effect reversal is the famous report of a dream that was felt to last a whole year.[17] The dreamer stated that he saw the beginning of the French Revolution, took part in all sorts of adventures, witnessed the terror and the execution of the King; he was jailed, interrogated, brought before the tribunal, convicted and sentenced to capital punishment, taken to the public square, put up on the block, and when the axe hit him on the neck—he awoke in horror, only to discover that the headboard of his iron cot had collapsed and struck him. From the beginning of the revolution (a) to the guillotine (x) the string is logically correct. The collapsing of the bed (the waking event omega) and the guillotine (the waking event x) are one and the same cause, interpreted differently by two states of consciousness belonging to two different planes of existence. In other words, by the daytime logic, the dénouement event x would lead to *alpha* (that is, be the initial cause of it), not the other way round.

16. F. W. Hildebrandt, *Der Traum und seine Verwertung für Leben*, 37ff. Freud often quotes from this book, approvingly, in his *Deutung*, although he cannot, of course, accept Hildebrandt's moral imperative.

17. Alfred Maury, *Le sommeil et les rêves*, 161. Freud recounts this dream as well, but in less detail.

. . . one little push
and down the white and handless face
of time—oh, lightly—down the side
of chimeless time and slimeless space,
oh, lightly shall we slide.

(from Nabokov's diary)[18]

1.

No matter its philosophical merits, Dunne's conception of "serial Time"—time that multiplies, as it were, upon itself in perpetuity—is in certain peculiar accord with Nabokov's own treatment of time in his compositions. Nabokov's experiment opened his last series of fictions, all written in Montreux; indeed, his very next novel, *Ada* (1968)—whose clockwork mechanism resides in the seminal part 4, "The Texture of Time," drafted in 1959—was likely set in motion by that "dream" experiment; it "started to flow," as he put it in his pocket diary about a year after the end of the experiment. And in the last part of the book Nabokov touches upon the question of the time vector in dreamland, cracking in passing at Freud's hollow symbolism (". . . a very amusing anti-Signy pamphlet on Time in Dreams").[19]

In later years, Nabokov would occasionally write down his dreams upon awakening, usually in his annual agenda books, even if he woke up in the middle of the night, more or less abiding by the "experiment" conditions as set by Dunne.

Nabokov's records show clearly that at the beginning of the experiment he dutifully followed those rules, minding that the record be unaffected by interpretation, something that he might have particularly liked about the

18. Note under March 3, 1952. In Manuscript Box: "Notes for Work in Progress," Berg Collection, New York Public Library.

19. *Ada*, 579.

whole thing, given that he held nothing but contempt for Freud's crude oneirology. Instead, he followed Dunne's advice that one should concentrate upon the happenings in the following day or two, trying to discern the trace of the preceding dream episode. This is a most difficult task because, Dunne warns, "the waking mind refuses point-blank to accept the association between the dream and the subsequent event."

The other difficulty, that of recalling and retaining the dream, can be removed relatively simply: "A notebook and pencil is kept under the pillow and, immediately on waking, before you even open your eyes, you set yourself to remember the rapidly vanishing dream," Dunne instructs. Nabokov jotted down his dreams the way he did his novels—on small, lined Oxford cards whose growing stack he rubber-banded; it is therefore highly unlikely that this lifelong insomniac kept that stack of A6 cards under his pillow. On several occasions he seems to have taken up Dunne's very helpful prescription of not attempting to recollect the entire dream, nor yet a large chunk of it, but rather a single episode, but in as much detail as one can, or even just one detail, and larger parts will unfold obligingly, not unlike small chips of an eggshell first crumbling off under the peeling thumb, causing ever larger ones to come off next.

Dunne advises that one should pay close attention to minutiae that appear particularly outlandish to the waking eye. He further enjoins his readers not to think of anything else until the dream has been recorded. At the end of each day, he adds, one is to reread all the records since the beginning of the experiment. Obviously those rules (and there are many more) place high demands even on the eager dreamer, challenging his diligence. No wonder Nabokov's zeal slackens as the experiment wears on, and we see more blank-dream days. By mid-November his experiment is losing some of its steam and much of its original purpose: he is just recording, often not noticing the connections with earlier or subsequent events. In December, several days go unrecorded altogether, and as 1964 draws to a close so does the experiment.

2.

What can a Nabokov reader glean or learn from these records half a century later? On reading the batch, one publisher, a good Freudian by his own admission, remarked that he was disappointed—evidently by the dearth of material suitable for standard psycho-interpretation, something that Nabokov surely would not fail to double-underline if he were to publish the dreams himself (and there are strong indications that he at least toyed with the idea). Since for every good Freudian there must be a hundred bad ones, a few flinders will doubtless be spotted and put to analytical deciphering, in spite—or perhaps because—of the fact that Nabokov made it a point to spray prefaces to his English books with strong anti-Freudian repellent.

The most interesting aspects of Nabokov's experiment have less to do with proving Dunne's theory right, for it seems inconclusive in this regard, than with certain threads that an accustomed eye can detect but which, paradoxically, escaped the dreamer, either because he could not recognize a past event or because he could not make out a future one. Unlike the people who attempted the experiment on Dunne's bidding and his precise instructions—unlike his sister, for example—here was a man of a prodigiously strong, well-trained memory, who could recollect the shade of a color of a shadow that an apple cast on the white tablecloth fifty years earlier, an artist of an astonishing acuity of perception, a peerless collector of detail, gifted with an unmatched faculty for expressing what he remembered and observed in vivid images of utmost clarity: Dunne, who stresses that "a short record, full of details, would be of more value than a long one drafted in vaguer terms" (65), could not wish for a better-suited subject than Nabokov, whose dream records are often compact but filled with precise and astoundingly fresh details.

Yet, most remarkably, even Nabokov would often fail to make connections between what seems to the reader a staring resemblance to an event in his past life or fiction, let alone a future occurrence.

In one particularly striking instance, already on the second day of the experiment, Nabokov's dream produces a Russian woman who asks him how he "like[s] it here, in St-Martin." He corrects her, "Mentone not Martin,"[20] and in his note upon awakening jots down that "Mentone" was a "dream substitute for Montreux," where he had lived since 1961. He goes on to recall his stay in Menton in the late 1930s, and his old mistake of calling the nearby Cap Martin "St-Martin," then immediately allows a fresh slip by placing Mont St-Michel in Menton (it is about eight hundred miles away, in Normandy) while surely meaning the local Basilique Saint-Michel.

Two days later he records what he will call his "first incontestable success in the Dunne experiment" because he has "the absolutely clear feeling" that a film he watched on television three days after a certain dream was the *source* of that dream—"had the latter followed the former," he hastens to explain. What he fails to register is that his dream distinctly and closely followed two scenes in his 1939 short story "The Visit to the Museum": the dreamlike encounter of the narrator with the museum's director in his office, and the odd exhibits in the local museum that looked like spherical soil samples, the chief subject of his dream.

20. Nabokov usually spelled "Menton" the Italian way.

Now, the museum in that story is apparently the munici-pal museum in *Menton,* which Nabokov had visited twenty-five years prior to his dream. The *St-Martin Centre funéraire* in Vevey, above the Russian church of St. Barbara, is where Nabokov's body was to be cremated less than thirteen years later.

"His slips of the tongue are oracular," remarks an Ameri-can professor about his Russian colleague in *Pnin.* As noted earlier, Dunne in principle allows only a day or two for a dream to forecast the actual event (so as to anticipate an objection stemming from probability theory); later he ac-cedes that "this might be extended in ration to the oddity and unusualness of the incident." He cites his dream of the 1916 bombardment of Lowestoft preceding the event by a year, and one clear case of a dream-image relating beyond all possibility of doubt to an event that happened some twenty years later: as a twelve-year-old boy Dunne had a dream affected by reading Jules Verne's *Clipper of the Clouds.* In that dream the flying apparatus had no wings, just small propellers. He remembered it only in 1910, when he piloted his ardis-shaped airplane "which possessed complete in-herent stability." It soared over the aerodrome, "steady as a rock" (the engine gave out three minutes later, a usual mishap at the time).

But while Dunne's serial Time theory makes some room for a dream to come true sometimes years later, it certainly pays no heed to a postmortem possibility—something that Nabokov, on the other hand, would be thrilled to consider. It is utterly difficult for the dreamer to connect a dream, even a recorded one, to a later event in life, but extending a dream pointer beyond life's terminus seems impossible. Nabokov could recall, however vaguely, his "experimental" dream, then check the written record of it, eight years later, when Anna Feigin, his wife's cousin and a close friend, in the care of the Nabokovs in her twilight years, died and was cremated at St-Martin's funeral facility.[21] He might ponder, on that occasion, the likely possibility of his own body's future visit there. He left no trace of either in his diary, although in at least one instance he did go back to his records and added a later comment (Dream 2). It is somewhat harder to understand Nabokov's failing to see a connection, sometimes direct, to his past life and writing. In a record of an earlier dream (Jan. 11, 1951; see part 3) he writes that he can't explain its setting—Rumania, revolution, the Queen—inexplicably failing to recall that his grandmother went to Bucharest on an invitation by the Queen of Rumania.

3.

In an experiment done upon oneself, one is at once the object and the subject of it: both a character (dreamer) and the author (dream writer and translator). Nabokov tries this sort of thing in his very last and unfinished novel, *The Origin of Laura*, in which a psychology professor takes up an experiment that entails the gradual erasing of himself by corradiated mental energy, all the while setting down its stages (and much more). In that sense Dunne's experiment proved, in one philosophical aspect, to be quite similar to the premise and condition of Nabokov's fiction, for it was, like one of his novels, a life experiment on a small scale, in which the experimenter turns into a *persona dramatis* for whom it is extremely

21. Nabokov notes in his diary for January 10, 1973: "*Inhumation des cendres de M. Anna Feigin dans la concession cinéraire no. 1232, piquet c. 317. Echéance de la concession 10 Janvier 2003* (that figure *fait rêver*)." [Interment of the ashes of Miss Anna Feigin in the cinerarium plot no. 1232, marker 317. Expiration 10 January 2003 (a dreamlike figure)]. See p. 70, note 58. By a curious, if absurd, coincidence, a different combination of the same numbers 0–1–2–3 in the plot number and the next century year of the concession's expiration, so hard to picture in 1973, was in Nabokov sister's Geneva address: 1203, 32 rue des Charmilles.

difficult to go back and reread his life, let alone to leap ahead. And much as the reader of his fiction can leaf back scores of pages to find an earlier forking episode in the character's life path, so the reader of Nabokov's dream records can easily move back and forth in time, with no temporal constraints, recalling this or that scene in his prior or future life or book. This is precisely the relation of the author-reader, on the one plane, and characters, on another, that Nabokov invented and cultivated.[22] The dream experiment of this sort offers an instructive analogy, sometimes affording an observer the privilege of seeing more than even the dreamer of Nabokov's prodigious memory and phenomenal imagination could.

Nabokov certainly did believe in predictive dreams prior to reading Dunne's book or undertaking his "experiment," and left records of some of his dreams in diaries and letters. They usually had to do with persons close to him. His parents, especially his father, were familiar visitors, and the reader of his "experiment" dream (no. 38), and of a similar earlier one (see part 3, Dream II), will recall dreams of similar tone and mood that the hero of *The Gift* has of *his* father, who in many ways is an expeditionary version of Nabokov's statesman father, exploring the world's deepest mysteries with butterfly net in hand.

Nabokov could not avoid translating his vaguely prevision-ary dreams into the hyperobjective language of waking life. Some records are verbal wonders, the most amazing of which came in two installments separated by decades; Dunne would gladly publish a new edition of his *Experiment* just to include them. In a 1916 dream, the seventeen-year-old Nabokov saw his uncle, who had died very shortly before leaving him a large fortune (swept away a year later in the revolutionary

22. For more on this important aspect of Nabokov's fiction, see Gennady Barabtarlo, "Nabokov's Trinity: On the Movement of a Nabokov Theme," 109–38.

maelstrom). In a matter-of-fact mutter, Uncle Basil said what sounded like typically lucid somnolent nonsense: "I shall come back to you as Harry and Kuvyrkin."[23] Forty-two years thereafter that dormant image gave off a flash of perfect sense when Harris and Kubrick Pictures approached Nabokov with an attractive offer of a handsome sum to buy the film rights to *Lolita*, at once restoring much of his lost fortune half a century later, half a world away. This is an inconceivable example of what may be termed, adapting Florensky's bold proposition, a reverse perspective of time-space wherein causality is reversed, so that Nabokov's dream was, in that dimension of sense, not the cause but the *effect* of Kubrick's "later" episode, in perfect agreement with Dunne's serialism. Furthermore, the sheer functionality of this very verbal dream is stupendous, and if it did not come from a diary entry one might suspect that it was fabricated to fit artistic application. Not only does this dream display an exceedingly rare triple convergence (the overall meaning and the similar shape of *both* pairs of names), not only does *kuvyrok* mean somersault in Russian, but it has an additional linguistic twist: the "Kuvyrkin to Kubrick" transformation proceeds with the correct sound shift from the Slavonic to the Latin.[24]

In 1939 Nabokov writes to his wife (from London to Paris): "This morning I was awoken by an unusually vivid dream: Il'usha (I think it was he)[25] walks in and says that he has been informed by phone call that Khodasevich has *'ended his earthly existence'*—word for word."[26] This was written on

23. Boyd-1991, 366.
24. The Latin bilabial *beta* stands for the Byzantine, and thus Slavonic, labiodental "v" (as in Barbara–Varvara, Basil–Vasily etc.).
25. Ilya Fondaminsky (1880–1942), Nabokov's close friend, a former member of the Russian Socialist-Revolutionary party; after the Bolshevik coup d'état he emigrated to Paris.
26. Vladislav Khodasevich (1886–1939), Russian poet, also a friend of Nabokov's; *Letters to Véra*, 434; translation slightly edited.

June 9; Khodasevich died on the 14th, and even though he had been ill for some time and in a hospital since late May, there was no indication of a rapidly approaching end until the surgery four days after Nabokov had seen him in that dream, hundreds of miles away.

On December 8, 1945, he writes to Mark Aldanov, a fellow writer and friend, concerning his brother Sergey: ". . . Just before I received word that he perished,[27] I had seen him in a terrible dream, lying on the bunk and gasping for air, convulsing in agony."[28] Twenty years later Nabokov would ponder the exciting possibility that time could turn itself inside-out—that the October 1945 letter from his sister, telling him of their brother's death, informed his *preceding* dream, rather than the more common explanation of the dream forestalling the terrible news.

4.

Nabokov's experiment had a peculiar complication that Dunne did not foresee. All his life he struggled with insomnia that required, especially during the last period in Montreux, nightly use of strong medication. As his Swiss doctors prescribed increasingly more powerful sleeping pills, Nabokov covered the pages of his pocket agenda books with the names, potency, dosages, even shape and color of the pills. As we know, dreams occur during the so-called rapid eye movement stage, in transition from the deep to the shallow stages of sleep ("paradoxical sleep"), near the surface.

27. In January 1945, in the German Neuengamme concentration camp near Hamburg. See Dieter Zimmer's definitive account, "What Happened to Sergey Nabokov?" (2015).

28. The Bachmetev Archive, New York. Aldanov Papers, Box 6. Quoted, in my translation, from Galina Glushanok's article in *Vladimir Nabokov: Pro et Contra* (St. Petersburg: Russian Christian Institute for the Humanities, 2001), 112.

Nabokov typically remembered having his dreams at dawn, right before awakening after a sleepless night, with much tossing and frequent getting up.

How does the fact that an elderly subject of a dream experiment—suffering as Nabokov did from sleeplessness and an enlarged prostate gland (it had to be removed ten years later)—who wakes up many times during the night, thereby frequently interrupting the sleep cycle, work on the character of his dreams? Does a strong chemical intervention affect their content? And above all, how do these factors bear upon the main purpose of Dunne's experiment—to prove that Time, like other dimensions of our universe, is not bound by the forward direction alone? In a chance ditty Nabokov jotted down in his pocket book on November 21, 1972, a wan smile overlays the pain:

Вставалъ, ложился опять.
  Заря какъ смертъ приближалась.
Если дальше не буду спать,
  Я пожалуюсь.

[Got up, lay down, got up again.
  Daybreak, like death, drew nearer, creeping.
If I'll keep going on without sleeping,
  I shall complain.]

In the remaining five years of his life such notes filled the pages of his agenda, in the last year crowding out most other items.

April 20 [1973] For the first time *in years* (since 1955? 1960?): Had this night a six-hour stretch of uninterrupted sleep (12–6). My usual extent of sleep (apart from periodical insomnias), even if induced by more or less potent pills (at least thrice daily) is a 3+2+1 or at best 4+2+2 or at frequent worst 2+1+1+2+1-hour affair with intervals (+) of hopelessness and nervous urination. This night I took an innocuous "mogadon" pill.[29]

Getting up just once is an extreme rarity, secured by a strong drug:

September 11 [1974] Motolon seems to work.[30]

September 12 9–12, 1–9, 1 WC. Best night in my life.

But once a habit was formed, a new medication had to be found. Sleep disorder is a mild professional euphemism for his condition. A year later he makes this account of his nightly ordeal:

August 21 [1975]: Sample of "good" night. Fell asleep around 8.45 slept till 8.45 with the following toilet interruptions at

10.05 PM
11.05
12.35
1.40 AM
2.20
3.45
5.35
6.20
8.45

Ten days later:

29. Known also as Insomin or nitrazepam—a pretty potent hypnotic, hardly innocuous.
30. Methaqualone, "a nonbarbiturate compound formerly used as a sedative and hypnotic, now found only as a drug of abuse" (*Miller-Keane Encyclopedia of Medicine*, 2003).

September 1 [1975]: First really good night
Bed 9, WC 11, 12. Slept. 4.45 WC. 7 up

How odd to compare these torments with his early years, when sleeplessness might look poetically enticing:

> . . . какъ прекрасно, какъ лучезарно порой прерывается міровое однообразіе книгой генія, кометой, преступленіемъ или даже просто одной ночью безъ сна.

[how splendidly, how radiantly the world's monotony is interrupted now and then by the book of a genius, a comet, a crime, or even simply by a single sleepless night.] ("La Veneziana")[31]

The situation was further complicated by Nabokov's efforts not to disturb his wife in the adjacent bedroom— yet sometimes the fear of "death creeping up close" over-whelmed him. On April 24, 1976, the day after his seventy-seventh birthday, he "woke up at 1 AM in panic of the this-is-it sort, discreetly screaming so as not to wake up her and yet to wake her up."

Nabokov's eighty-night experiment in the fall of 1964 was a sustained effort to study his fragmented, ungraspable dream-life under the daylight supposition that time is reversible. This supposition undergirds a number of Nabokov's fictional writings, including, perhaps not so paradoxically, his mem-oirs. It reaches its climax in his last complete novel, *Look at the Harlequins!*, whose hero takes his inability to spatialize time by reversing it for a form of insanity. Part 5 of this book puts to study some interesting aspects of Nabokov's singular treatment of time in his fiction.

31. *Stories*, 105.

In a sense, Nabokov conducted a lifelong nightly experiment with Time, under a condition where the term "chronic" reclaims its original meaning and extends Time into and beyond the philosophical realm, into the hereafter, which Nabokov studied in life and fiction, day and night, and where "there should be time no longer."

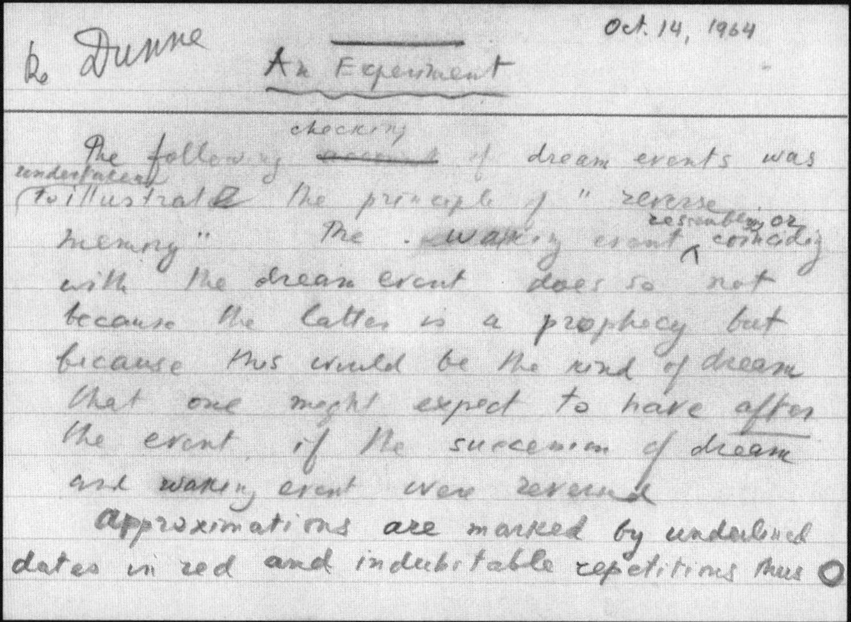

R. Dunne

An Experiment

Oct. 14, 1964

The following ~~account~~ checking of dream events was undertaken to illustrate the principle of " reverse memory." The waking event resembling or coinciding with the dream event does so not because the latter is a prophecy but because this would be the kind of dream that one might expect to have after the event, if the succession of dream and waking event were reversed

Approximations are marked by underlined dates in red and indubitable repetitions thus ○

FIGURE 3. The first day of the experiment.

PART 2

DREAMER'S LOG

During the process of writing I was under the impression that
I was turning out something very smart and witty; on occasions
a like thing happens in dreams: you dream you are making a
speech of the utmost brilliancy, but when you recall it upon
awakening, it goes nonsensically: "Besides being silent before
tea, I'm silent before eyes in mire and mirorage," etc.

—Vladimir Nabokov, *Despair*

Oct. 14, 1964

An Experiment

The following checking of dream events was undertaken to illustrate the principle of "reverse memory."[1] The waking event resembling or coinciding with the dream event does so not because the latter is a prophecy but because this would be the kind of dream that one might expect to have *after* the event. If the succession of dream and waking event were reversed, approximations are marked by underlined dates in red and indubitable repetitions thus: ⊕.[2]

---

1. Some of Nabokov's spelling idiosyncrasies, such as omitting the apostrophe in "don't," were left alone; some inconsistencies ("gray" / "grey" on the same card) have been normalized; obvious pencil slips have been corrected silently.

2. Dunne marks "singly decisive results" with a plus sign; those "nearly decisive" with a circled cross, which he calls a "sort of hot-cross-bun." VN does not

Types of dreams[3]

---

1. Professional & vocational (in my case: literature, teaching, and lepidoptera).
2. Dim-doom dreams (in my case, fatidic-sign nightmares: thalamic calamities, menacing series and riddles).
3. Obvious influences of immediate occupations & impressions (Olympic games etc.).
4. Memories of the remote past (childhood, émigré life, school, parents).
5. "Precognitive."
6. Erotic tenderness and heart-rending enchantment.

Curious features of my dreams:

---

1. Very exact clock time awareness but hazy passing-of-time feeling.
2. Many perfect strangers—some in almost every dream.
3. Verbal details.
4. Fairly sustained, fairly clear, fairly logical (within special limits) cogitation.
5. Great difficulty in recalling a complete dream even in outline.
6. Recurrent types and themes.

In connection with Dunne's book.

---

follow this system for long, soon bungles it by simply circling a few dates, then abandons it altogether. My occasional commentaries under an entry are marked by a red square.

3. These are on the recto and verso of an undated card inserted toward the end of the experiment, between records of December 6 and 7 in the extant batch, thus likely a postfactum summation.

Both running on asphalt (of street), Vé. behind.[4] About to overtake (easily) a horse-drawn carriage. I ask myself, and her (but she is now no longer behind) on which side does a runner overtake a carriage? A stranger in the cab (round face, oldish) asks me in Russian (or German?) am I well off? Criticizes my clothes (those I wear to-day). I explain that the spots on my trousers (which are somewhat browner than any I wear to-day) are due to my splashing across a puddle. Cannot find the way to, or remember the name of, a certain square in Berlin <VERSO> where Vé. (now apparently somehow in front) wants to visit a museum.[5] (We had been to an exposition of modern painting, in Lausanne, *place* Beaulieu, a few days before, but the atmosphere in my dream is different).

In the course of the day I remembered the "in front-behind" part of the dream when we walked with Vé., *she* in front, *I* behind on the very narrow sidewalk along which, very close to us, fast cars were overtaking us. But we are pestered by the traffic daily.

⊕ Thursday Oct. 15, 8.00 AM Detail of dream **2.**

Russian woman, stranger, speaking in glass telephone booth. Afterwards a few words exchanged. No longer young, ambitious make-up, coarse Slavic features. Wonders how I knew she was Russian. I answer dream-logically that only Russian women speak so loud on the phone. Asks if I like it here, in

4. Vé (sometimes just V.) refers to VN's wife, Véra Nabokov, née Slonim (1902–1991).

5. Visiting a museum—a plot-carrying truss of one of VN's most significant short stories, "*Poseshchenie muzeia*" [The Visit to the Museum], 1939—is something of a theme in this series of dreams: cf. next and Dream 3.

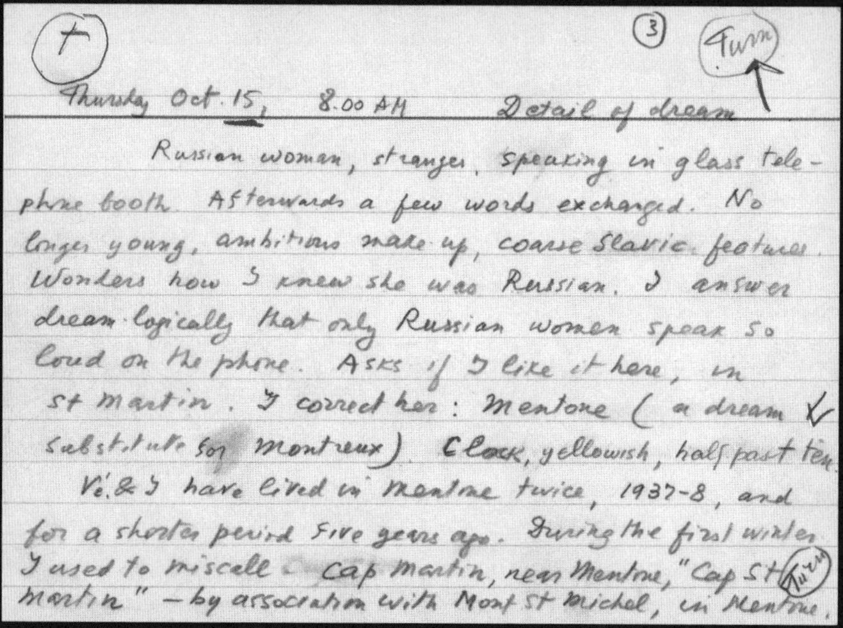

FIGURE 4. The ⊕ sign indicates that Nabokov thought this dream, seen already on the second day of the experiment, was of the "proleptic" sort, caused, as it were, by a later event. See page 22–23 for an interesting and surprising confirmation.

St-Martin. I correct her: Mentone (a dream substitute for Montreux). Clock, yellowish, half-past ten.[6]

Vé. & I have lived in Mentone twice, 1937–8, and for a shorter period five years ago. During the first winter I used to miscall Cap Martin, near Mentone, "Cap St Martin"—by association with Mont St Michel, in Mentone.[7]

<VERSO> ⊕ 11.45 same day

Reading Dunne's *An experiment with Time* came to the passage at the bottom of p. 100 (third edition) : . . . "the first image I saw and noted was a clock pointing to half-past-ten" (on which hangs the plot of a mystery story* *he* was using for an experiment—letting odds and ends of images come into the mind while thinking of the title of (or a name in) a book *before* reading it).

Evidence of "reverse memory"?

* Mason's *House of the Arrow*. [This is nice! Had quite forgotten this when inventing Ardis. March 4, 1968].[8]

6. See footnote 8.

7. Roquebrune-Cap-Martin, where Sebastian Knight assumes (wrongly) his mother died (*The Real Life of Sebastian Knight*, 1939). Mont St Michel is in Normandy, on the other end of France, about eight hundred miles from Menton. For the significance of this twofold slip of memory for VN's experiment, see pp. 22–23. Cf. the critical confusion of the church of St. Michel and that of Notre Dame in Dijon on the last page of *The House of the Arrow*—see next footnote.

8. *The House of the Arrow*, a 1924 novel by A. E. W. Mason. Here is a full quotation of that place: "I do not know if the present reader is acquainted with [it], and, if he is not, I am most unwilling to spoil for him, even in the interests of science, the enjoyment of a first-class detective story. So I will merely say that the centre knot of the whole tangle—the thing upon which everything in the plot hangs—*is a clock pointing to half-past ten*. This feature, however, does not come into the story till halfway through the book. The character I had chosen from the opening pages as an associational link accompanied the detective throughout the latter's investigation. Concentrating attention on that character, the first image I saw and noted was that of *a clock pointing to half-past ten*" (Dunne, 100, emphasis his). The character mentioned is Jim Frobisher, a young London solicitor. The book is indeed a first-rate example

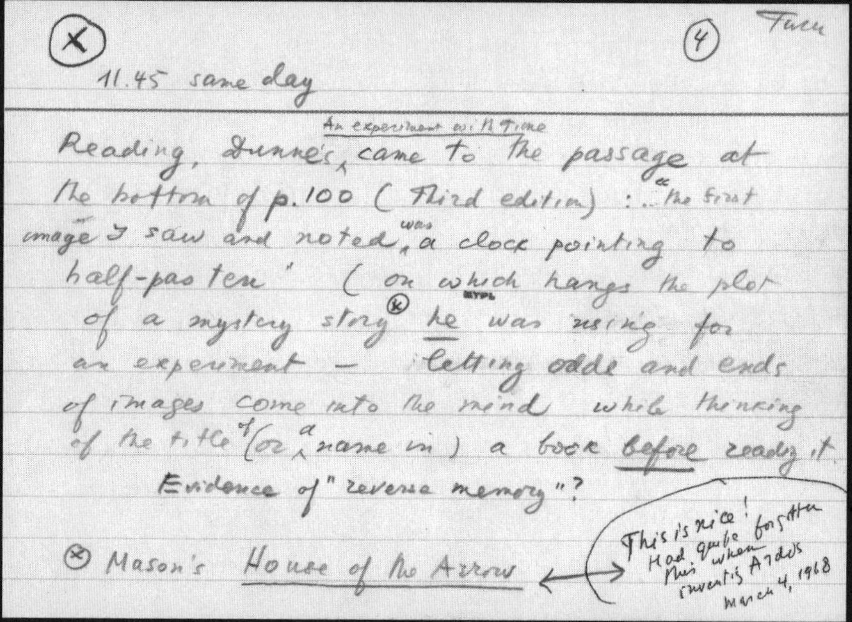

FIGURE 5. Another card, second in a row, marked as proving Dunne's premise. A curious 1968 note at the bottom shows that Nabokov reread the dream records while composing *Ada, or Ardor*. "Ardis" is the Greek for the tip of an arrow, hence the exclamation mark.

Dancing with Vé. Her open dress, oddly speckled and sum-
mery. A man kisses her in passing. I clutch him by the head
and bang his face with such vicious force against the wall that
he almost gets meat-hooked, on some fixtures on the wall
(gleaming metal suggestive of ship). Detaches himself with
face all bloody and stumbles away.

Thursday evening there was a reference on the TV to the
butchery and hanging of the participants in the bomb-plot
against Hitler.

17 Oct. 1964—8.30 AM (see Oct. 20)   **4.**

Sitting at round table in the office of the director of a small
provincial museum. He (a stranger, a colorless administra-
tor, neutral features, crewcut) is explaining something about
the collections. I suddenly realize that all the while he was
speaking I was absent-mindedly eating exhibits on the
table—bricks of crumbly stuff which I had apparently taken
for some kind of dusty insipid pastry but which were actually
samples of rare soils in the compartments (of which most are
now empty) of a tray-like wooden affair in which <VERSO>
geological specimens are kept. Although he had pointed at

---

of its kind, the most curious facet of which is that the chief sleuth, M. Hanaud, and
some critical turns are transferred from Dostoevsky's *Crime and Punishment* (except
that its deductive plot is replaced here by a detective one), some episodes appearing
almost as quotations from the earlier psycho-crime novel (such as the reconstruction
of the murder of Jean Cladel in chapter 17). It is unknown whether Nabokov read
Mason, but see note to the previous dream.

The main plot of VN's novel *Ada* (1968) unfolds on the country estate Ardis, the
Greek word for arrow point, but also a derivative of the Latin for "ardent," a ho-
mophonous echo (". . . *or Ardor*") of the book's title and one of its main themes. This
later note is evidence that Nabokov reread his dream records later, perhaps with the
view to preparing them for publication, an old idea of his: see pp. 2–3.

the tray while speaking, the director has not noticed yet anything wrong. I am now wondering not so much about the effects upon me of those (very slightly sugary) samples of soils but about the method of restoring them and what exactly they were—perhaps very precious, hard to procure, long kept in the museum (the labels on the empty compartments are reproachful but dim). The director is called to the telephone and <NEW CARD> [17 Oct. cont.] abruptly leaves the room. I am now talking to his assistant (German, wears glasses, youngish) who is very hard on the doctor who had been looking after me before I came to this clinic (ex-museum). In fact, that doctor's treatment (rather than the exhibits I have just consumed—which surely must aggravate my condition) has resulted in the possibility of an "iron-infection". He says I will be threatened by it at least during a whole year, will "live under the menace." <VERSO> He mispronounces this word as "mans" and turns apologetically and questioningly to the director of the clinic (who has now returned to his place at the table). The director whose native language is English nods and says "yes, there will be a mans." I correct him: *menace,* and am aware I have offended him.

(Quite recently—the day before yesterday—I had read of edible mushrooms, dry samples of which were offered, to be handled and sniffed at, to the visitors[9] to an exhibition. And last year we had been highly critical of one of D's doctors).[10]

■ *Nabokov calls this second day the "first incontestable success in the Dunne experiment," because he had "the absolutely clear feeling" that a TV film he watched three days after was the source of that dream—"had the latter followed the former," he hastens to explain (see Dream 7, October 20, 9.45). What he fails to recollect is that,*

9. The original has "*by* the visitors," surely a slip.
10. D (sometimes "Dm.") refers to Dmitri Nabokov (1934–2012), VN's son.

as recorded, his dream distinctly and closely followed two scenes in his 1939 short story "The Visit to the Museum," namely, the dream-logical encounter of the narrator with the museum's director in the latter's office and the strange exhibits in the local museum that looked like spherical soil samples, the chief subject of his dream. See also note to Dream 1.

Oct. 18, 1964 8.30 AM   **5.**

Several dreams which jostled each other out as I tried to remember; could only retrieve a few broken bits. A patch or pattern of ivy-like leaves or light-and-shadow with an after-image effect, suspended near me, was recognized as the fatidic sign of imminent dissolution: a "this-is-it" feeling, frequently experienced. Another dream, also recurrent, was the nightmare of finding myself in the haunts of interesting butterflies without my butterfly net and being reduced to capturing and messing up a rarity with my fingers—in this case a Spanish insect, a bleached Blue.

■ *A "lepidopterist of consequence," as another professional lepidopterist called him, Nabokov was a particular expert in the Blues family of butterflies. See footnote 41. The best assessment of the reciprocal relationship between his writing and his entomology can be found in the brilliant introductory essays by Brian Boyd and Robert Pyle to their book* Nabokov's Butterflies *(Boston: Beacon Press, 2000).*

Oct. 18, 1964—Evening

On TV: Olympics: runners (and walkers) splashing across puddles, all muddy, Vé. wonders how do they manage to overtake one another when bunched up. Compare dream of Oct. 14. Any connection?

6. Oct. 19, 1964—8.45 AM

Dream constipation continues. Managed to recall only one image, on the fringe of waking—hardly the dream itself, disjointed nothings, rudiments or dregs—namely a dim white propeller-like thing on a chair in a leafy avenue; and the words "Kars" (or "Kans") and "Etan," in another piece of dream stuff.

Webster says "Etana" was a Babylonian spaceman "who, attempting to mount to heaven on an eagle, became frightened and fell to his death."

7. Oct. 20, 1964—7.00 AM

Travel dream. Have just woken up in tawny-plush compartment of sleeping car, misty dawn in window on my right, green steel door of bathroom before me separating my compartment from Véra's (blend of European & American types of trains). Am surprised that had gone to sleep without the bed having been made, in a sitting corner position and fully dressed, and that the doors between us have remained closed. Suddenly realize, before even investigating my pockets, <VERSO> that my passport has remained where it always lies—in the left drawer of my desk in Montreux. In the meantime the train is approaching the border (apparently Belgium, which I crossed so often in the past). I ponder the question—shall I telephone to our concierge at the Palace Hotel to have him forward the thing? Shall I wake Vé.?

In a second instalment of the dream we have trouble finding our luggage at the customs.

■ *Long-distance trains were VN's boyhood special passion—see* chapter 7 of Speak, Memory.

Oct. 20, 1964—12.00 AM[11]

Read in the N.Y. Times about the death, in aircrash near Belgrade, of several Red Army officers. The plane hit a hill in the fog and one engine landed on a forest road that winds to the top of Avala Hill. Cp. dream jotted down yesterday. Good enough?

⊕ Oct. 20 9.45 PM, Tuesday

Turned on at 9 AM the TV (France), educational film, *Le Pédologue* (thought it was about children).[12] But pedology is also the science treating of soils. Three men (two Negro geologists & a French interviewer) were revealed seated around an ordinary table placed near a tent in the Senegal brush—and I immediately recalled my dream noted last Saturday, Oct. 17. The *échantillons de sols*[13] discussed by them were the samples of soils of that dream. The samples in appetizing little bags (*des sachets*) were presently brought in a wooden tray into a Dakar office where brick-like boxes of specimens lined the wall. The soils turned <VERSO> into eatables—vegetables and fruit collected by the natives. One of the pedologists spoke French with what sounded like a Russian accent. I would have looked at the film, anyway, because [I was] trying to glimpse butterflies in the several excellent views of the *brousse*.[14]

I note the absolutely clear feeling I had of this film being the source of my dream (had the latter followed the former).

11. Surely a slip (PM).
12. Because it looks exactly like the American spelling of *paedology*.
13. Soil samples.
14. Underbrush.

This is my first incontestable success in the Dunne experiment. Two or three less definite ones occurred in connection with dreams jotted down on Oct. 14, 15, & 19.

8. Oct. 21, 8 AM

Had rich and strange visions, remembered them between two abysses of sleep but now cannot recollect anything save some vague fragments of a trivial erotic dream. (Vé. tells me she saw a big elevator: seven people in it, with furniture, she talks to a German girl who complains she is ill-paid. Complicated details of ringing bells. Connected with a slow lift she used when visiting doctor in Geneva yesterday).

9. Jotted down at 8.30 AM—Oct. 22

Two fragments of Véra's dreams.

    a. Sports in Africa. Long necklace of black and white alternating, worn by one of the runners.
    b. We were representatives of Fiat. They met us rather coolly. They had built a white bungalow-like house for us. Figure 29 dominated the whole thing.

I gleaned only a communication at the moment of awakening that "Somnambule Bureau had been accused of malpractices."

10. Oct. 23—6.00 AM

Several dreams, a fragment of one recalled. Am in a kind of gym or barbershop. At some distance from me, Dm., wrapped up in sheet, is being massaged or having his hair cut. A phonograph is put on for him. It is a record I made to amuse him—I'm singing an aria (from Bor. Godunov, perhaps), but it is less funny than I had hoped, the tune is quite unrecognizable and even the "ha-ha" laugh into which I break off at the end sounds false.

■ *Dmitri Nabokov was an operatic basso profundo. He was to sing "Death of Boris," the star aria from Mussorgsky's* Boris Godunov, *three years after this dream. Nine years later, Nabokov wrote the liner notes for an album of the Russian songs and romances that his son recorded for BASF.*

8.00 AM: another dream

Trudging up a steep plank-laid way between boulders. Higher up, a sunny slope, in a Spanish town. Many butterflies flying <VERSO> about. A local lepidopterist introduces me to the fauna. With the dark common thing I catch, there is in my net a marvelously fresh specimen of a greatly enlarged and brightened *Triphysa phryne*—a subspecies of it unknown to me with a splendid orange flush around the ocelli. The local chap explains in English it is the progeny of a population imported from the steppes of S.E. Russia (There are several S. Russian butterflies represented in Spain, but *not* this species).

(Since the beginning of the month we have been toying with the idea of going in spring to S. Spain).

Oct. 23—8.15 AM

(Véra's dream.

Certain Olympics participants, found them<selves?> very far out in the ocean—perhaps shipwrecked. They were forced, on purpose or by circumstances, to swim shoreward. Although the officials had no right to let them be even seen, let alone rewarded, they still were, illegally, listed as have performed in the Olympics).

11.   Saturday, Oct. 24, 1964 8.00 AM

The fact of being able to retrieve only the very end of a long interesting dream is most annoying:
V. & I are seeing Dm. off. We are standing at the tram stop and looking at the tramcar he has just boarded. We can't see him but presently hear him lustily singing inside. I realize that he is placed somehow above the occupants of the car—they are looking up with appreciative expressions on their faces. I climb upon some kind of stand to see him, but am unable to do so.

(Dm. is taking part in autom<obile> races in Italy this afternoon & to-morrow).

Oct. 24—8.30 AM

(Véra's dreams :

1. We are shown a film of a jumping match between two countries one of which is African and begin<s> with M. It turns out to be the performance of a play of mine, with Brialy.[15]

2 and 3 mingled: a town where it was impossible to find a taxi. We were finally given one with its keys and no driver. A hotel room with a chest of (4) drawer<s> and two faucets on top: one could take a bath in the third drawer from the top. She let the water run & <VERSO> got in the back of taxi to clean the window or something. A couple comes up and wants to take the taxi. The woman reminds her of a person she knew years ago in Cambridge, Mass. She tells her it is not a taxi for rent, then remembers the running faucets and goes upstairs. They threaten to find the man who owns the taxi. She is aware that all the drawers must be very wet though only the *lower* one is being

---

15. Jean-Claude Brialy (1933–2007), French cinematic actor born in Algeria.

filled with water. The couple, and the landlady, come up. The former want the keys of the car. V. says she won't give them. They say, who has a key: Well, Miss Shapiro (the housekeeper) will drive us. V. wants to telephone to get the key back. All this against the background of a big ocean liner—possibly on board.

■ *Curiously, a number of verbs in this note ("are," "begins," "turns") were at first written in the past tense, then changed to the dramatic present.*

Oct. 25, 1964 9.30   **12.**

Slept much longer than usual, woke up with neuralgia—and only a very dim recollection of several dreams. The influence of the Olympics TV pictures on V's and my dreams lately is quite obvious. It was combined this time with a familiar nightmare accompanying neuralgia in the temple: dim gloomy riddles which I must solve in a kind of dreadful "quiz" involving the necessity to memorize sequences of more or less abstract, insipid, ragged images, surds and shadows of surds.[16]

Oct. 26, 1964. Blank[17]   **13.**

Oct. 27, 1964. 8.30 AM   **14.**

Several vivid dreams besides some tender erotic stuff and a fatidic-sign nightmare (flags ascending very olympically, one of them meaningfully Turkish). The word "Synecampus."

16. A mathematical term (Latin translation of the original Arabic for "inaudible") for a certain kind of irrational number (e.g., the square root of two). In *Pnin*, Nabokov uses it as shorthand for an intellectually attractive eccentric.
17. "A dreamless sleep is an illusion of memory," quoth Dunne (64).

Memorized final fragments of two long dreams: V. urges me to hurry as we escape from a hotel (not this one) in the middle of the night. Helps me to find my blue raincoat. We rush out and she instantly vanishes. Vast hotel grounds, artistically bathed in diffuse moonlight, everything flaky and fluid, dim outlines of shrubs, dim figures, children still-out-so-late, a miniature dachshund, the sonorous voices of a party of Russians <VERSO> taking leave of one another in the darkness beyond the moonlight. I decide to wait for V. and sit down on the gravel; sitting beside me is a fat youngish Russian, a stranger in a grey suit. Some ceremony is about to take place and he tells me that as a political gesture we'd better stand up to attention. I peevishly refuse, he stands up alone, is angry, threatens me. I take the stick of my butterfly net, light metal, vulcanized handle, and attack him. He flinches and crouches with his back to me, groping for his thick cane which is tipped with iron. I strike him across the shoulder blades—not quite the tremendous whack I intended, but still quite a rap.

14-A. Oct. 27, 1964 8.30 AM, cont.

The other fragment same night (27 Oct., 1964): have called on M. Kalashnikov, a friend of the early 20-ties (whose farcical personality must be described some day).[18] He is staying with a titled Russian family, in a large rambling house. We sit down to a rambling dinner, lots of people, I do not know anybody, am bored and exasperated. M. K., a little apart, gloomily consumes a thick red steak, holding it rather daintily, the nails of his long fingers glisten with cherry-red varnish. I get up and wander away. Failed to memorize the

---

18. A scathing sketch of Mikhail Kalashnikov, VN's onetime classmate at Cambridge, can be found in his letter to Wilson (*Nabokov–Wilson*, 181). He is also mentioned in *Speak, Memory* (259).

long middle. The setting has analogies with the past but the details of the last scene have none.

Oct. 28, 1964 6.00 AM   **15.**

A long dream which I can only recall vaguely. It is a lecture room dream and I am the lecturer. Cannot decipher my notes, fuzzy lines with illegible corrections, murky insertions, messy deletions. (This type of dream is really not so much an echo of my lectures at American colleges, as a much older, disguised, recollection of my not knowing the lesson as a schoolboy— dreams that continued to haunt me well into my thirties).

■ *Cf. "But alas, even when you do happen, in a dream, to make such a return journey, then, at the border of the past your present intellect is completely invalidated, and amid the surroundings of a classroom hastily assembled by the nightmare's clumsy property man, you again do not know your lesson—with all the forgotten shades of those school throes of old"* (The Gift, *54) and "the recurrent dream we all know (finding ourselves in the old classroom, with our homework not done because of our having unwittingly missed ten thousand days of school)"* (Bend Sinister, *55).

Oct. 28, 1964 8.30 AM, same morning   **15-A.**

V. and I are on our way to Wellesley where I have to deliver the first lecture of the year—and my first lecture at that college.[19] At the railway station somewhat resembling South station in Boston, but then degenerating into a Swiss station. I linger near a newspaper stand, while V., who has the tickets, hurries onto the platform. I look at the clock

19. VN taught at Wellesley College as an untenured lecturer of Russian from 1941 to 1947.

and see it is 12.10: I have fourteen minutes. I cannot find the paper I want and decide to try the stand on the platform but when I arrive at the gate I realize V. has my ticket. The two <VERSO> men at the gate refuse to let me through, refuse to be bribed, and tell me to go back to the nearest ticket-office. Happily I know where to find it, right, left, and right again. It is 12.20 when I reach it. Two or three fat nuns are before me, but I manage to push through into a small room with a counter. The man suspiciously inquires why I am in such a hurry. "Are you a medecine?" (*médecin*). I say no and urge him to go on with my ticket which is a booklet the blanks of which he has to fill in. He says that if I were <NEW CARD>

Oct. 28, 1964 8.30 AM, cont.

a doctor I would have known I should comply with the instructions on "bacteria" in one of the sections of the ticket. He starts to cross out the sentence, remarking he hopes the conductor will still let me get on the train. I am now in a rage and tell him I am "an American Subject". The clock-hand is now at 12.23, and jerks forward as I look. I shout at him it is now too late, he comes out from behind the counter, and <I> kick him before rushing out. I am now in despair: what has V. done: has she boarded the train? Will she find me? Greatly relieved it is only a dream.

■ *This familiar type of nightmare—being late to a train, mad haste in slow-motion, fairy-tale obstacles—is rather frequent in VN's writing: see especially* The Real Life of Sebastian Knight, *and note to Dream 23, November 5.*

The verso of this card has a working note, unrelated to the experiment, headed by the instruction to self ("Rewrite") and later crossed out:

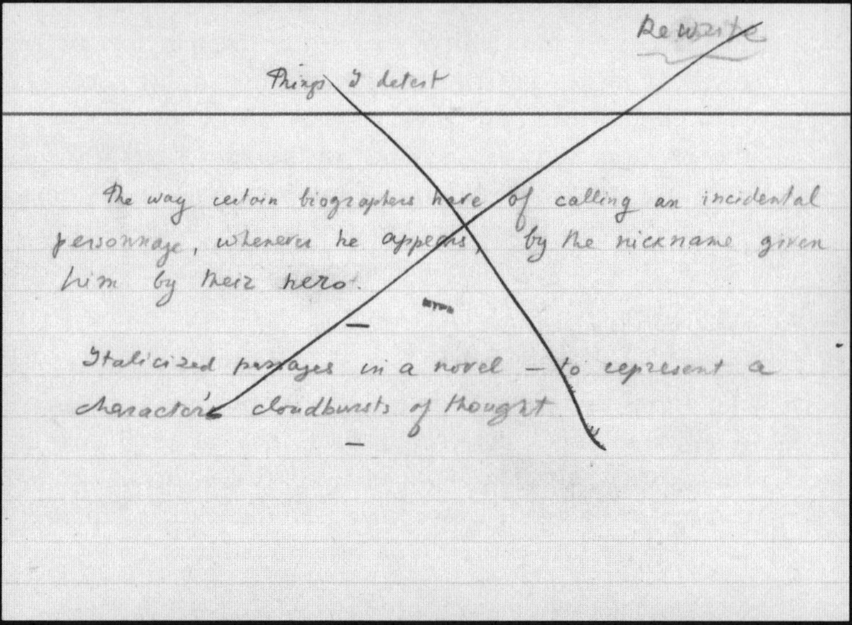

FIGURE 6. Verso of a card describing dream 15-A (October 28, 8.30 AM).

The way certain biographers have of calling an incidental personage, whenever he appears, by the nickname given him by their hero.

Italicized passages in a novel—to represent a character's cloudbursts of thought.

Oct. 28, 1964 9.30 same morning

Remembered a frayed bit of yet another dream at the moment I was taking out my sponge from its bag hanging above the bath. In that dream I had become aware that I now noticed for the first time a kind of sack modestly hiding among the towels near the bath where as I now realized Mme Cavin, the woman who cooks for us, leaves her things when she comes—ah, that's where! (not an actual arrangement, of course!)

16. Oct. 29, 1964 8.30 AM

(V.'s dream, a retrieved fragment. We are all to dine with Sonia[20] who lives in a pension owned by the French consul who closely supervises it. Since he is one of S.'s guests, someone says we can be sure of a good dinner and S. affirms it will be carefully prepared but very simple. A dachshund participated.)

17. Oct. 30, 1964—8.00 AM Nothing

18. Oct. 31—8.00 AM

Among several dreams was a really stunning recollection of early childhood. I was again immersed in these dreadful tantrums, those storms of tears with which my mother had to cope

20. Sophia Slonim, the younger sister of VN's wife (1908–1996).

when I was 4–5 years of age and we were abroad. The dream beautifully brought back the sensation of utter disaster when letting myself completely go I simultaneously realized that I was removing further and further, with every sob, and howl a reconciliation with my helpless, distraught mother. In tonight's dream, I was <NEW CARD> already in such a tempest as I rushed from my and S.'s[21] bedroom in a hotel into the white corridor and endeavored to break into mother's room. She would not let me in—cried out abruptly and jarringly that she was trying on something. I dashed into a water closet and next moment was oddly standing on the lid and hugging the white-washed pipe that went *upward* to a basin-like affair in which I plunged my face (the dream rather eccentrically gave the measure <NEW CARD> of my *height* by means of this position which apparently had no other purpose or meaning). My mother with bright eyes and flushed face opened the door at the end of a kind of vestibule leading to the place where I sobbed. There I let myself go completely. Unfortunately at this moment my brother S. whom the English governess was dressing heard my sobbing and joined in. This double performance spoilt the matter and M.[22] instead of consoling me broke into tears herself.

Had been rereading (Oct. 29) the Russian version of *Speak, Memory*.[23]

Nov. 1, 1964 8.30 AM[24]   *19.*

Many dreams, among them one erotic vision, then a long rambling dream: am coming home at noon with butterfly net. On

21. Here the initial stands for Sergey Nabokov, VN's younger brother (1900–1945). See p. 27, note 27.
22. Elena Nabokov, née Rukavishnikov, Nabokov's mother (1876–1939).
23. In 1954 Nabokov revised and translated into Russian his autobiography (*Speak, Memory*, originally *Conclusive Evidence*, 1951) under the title *Drugie berega* (Other Shores).
24. The original has "Oct. 1," a slip of the pen.

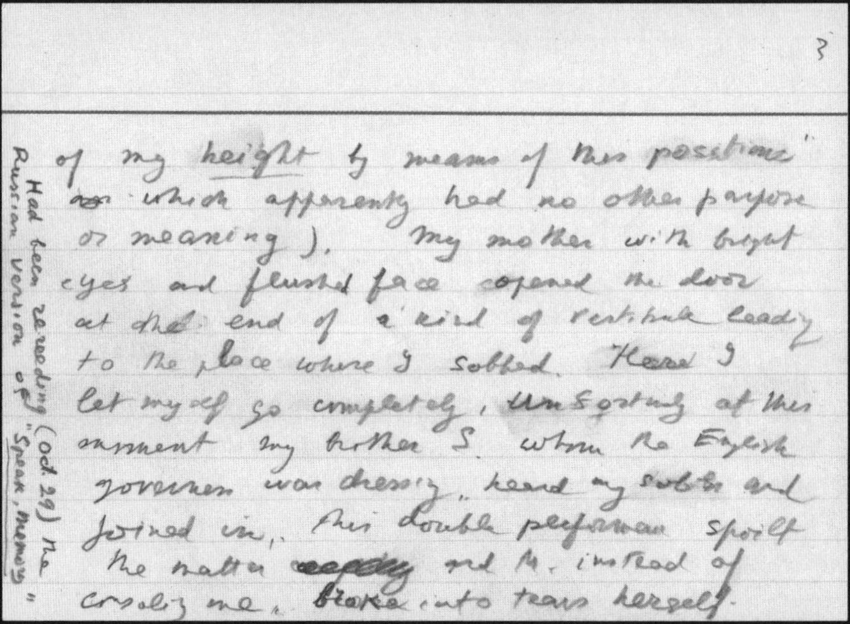

3

of my height by means of this position'
nor which apparently had no other purpose
or meaning).   My mother with bright
eyes and flushed face opened the door
at the end of a kind of vestibule leading
to the place where I sobbed. Here I
let myself go completely, unsporting at this
moment my brother S. whom the English
governess was dressing, heard my sobs and
joined in, this double performance spoilt
the matter ~~completely~~ and M. instead of
consoling me, ~~broke~~ into tears herself.

Had been re-reading (Oct 29) the Russian version of "Speak, Memory"

FIGURE 7. The third card recording the dream on October 31.

my left, through sparse wood across grass, across paths walks woman in white talking to herself and humming—resembling the lady who kept trying to waylay me in the neighborhood of Loèche-les-Bains,[25] summer 1963. A kind of short causeway on my right leads me out of the grove to the opposite side of the valley where after a rond-point the path ends at the door of pink-brick villa V. & I have rented; but the door is locked, I do not have the key. I ponder how to get in and wake up. Landscape quite unknown to me.

Nov. 2, 1964 6.30 AM   **20.**

Several dreams in succession as usual, last one dimly recollected: Dm. and I are trying to track down a repulsive plump little boy who has killed another child—perhaps his sister.

— — 8.00 AM

Somehow am unable to find the Museum of Comparative Zoology at Harvard.[26] Seem to have got out at the wrong underground station. Upon entering a building find several people conversing in Russian in a kind of entrance hall. I surprise them by addressing them in Russian. One of them— <VERSO> a small frail man (funny how many of my dream characters are perfect strangers!) whom I ask to direct me, replies it's at least half an hour's walk—though I know it must be just round the corner. He says he had "big unpleasantnesses" (in Russian)[27] at the MCZ which he had just visited on business (and at this point, i.e. long before waking, I have

25. An ancient Swiss thermal spa in canton Valais. Dmitri Nabokov was treated in Rheumaklinik there from May to August of 1963.
26. VN worked there as a research fellow and de facto curator of lepidoptera from 1942 to 1948.
27. A literal translation of the idiomatic Russian for contretemps (*nepriyatnosti*).

briefly the eerie feeling that I should write down all this! The Dunne Interference![28]) He also refers to a Professor Lag— unknown to me, offers to walk thither with

<NEW CARD> Nov. 2, 1964 8.00 AM, continued.

me and puts on his pointed karakul shapska.[29] I say I think I'll manage alone and start to go. But the exit is now a trap-door or roofdoor—opens up, does not stay up, cannot wriggle through (have a parcel), some old rag falls from top as I try to adjust the frame—and here I wake up.

(One of my "professional" dreams, but also connected with the difficulty I have these days in settling the location of specimens at the Nat. Hist. Mus. (B.M.) which I need for my book on European butterflies.).[30]

21.   Nov. 3, 1964 9.00 AM

(Woke up much later than usual, recalled end of dream) After grave illness put on hurriedly white flannel trousers and dark blue jacket with the intention of bicycling to the end of our park where my cousin Yuric (he was killed in 1919 and

28. VN probably means "intervention": "As the result of observing an image of future experience, the experimenter takes pencil and paper, and notes down, or even makes a sketch of, the details of the pre-image observed. In so doing, he is performing a definite physical act. *But it is an act which would never have been performed had he not observed that pre-image.* In other words, he interferes with that particular sequence of mechanical events which we postulate as the backbone of our 'conscious automaton' or materialistic theories. This is barefaced 'intervention'" (105–6, italics Dunne's).

29. A hat of black, tightly curled sheep fur.

30. From September 1963 to August 1965 Nabokov worked on *The Butterflies of Europe,* his unfinished book project intended for publication by Weidenfeld & Nicolson. His letters, drafts, and notes on the matter are in *Nabokov's Butterflies* (569ff.). He intended to do research, among other depositories and libraries, at London's Museum of Natural History and the British Museum.

I am fifteen in my dream)[31] is cycling. Deliberate with myself should I take my butterfly net. Decide not to. Am wearing white shoes with heels. Rush down to dining room (of Vyra house[32]) to eat something, but it is late, the table has been cleared of breakfast. Find some fruit in vase on side board, take a banana after making sure there is one left for Dm. Nice blend!

Nov. 4, 1964 9.00 AM   **22.**

Again slept late. Several dreams, both V's and mine, irretriev-able (or, as she says "tried in vain to pull one of them out by the end of the thread"). Just before waking saw on my right (I always sleep on the right side[33]) one of my "fatidic signs", this time a thick orange-red spiral on a dull brown field—the blazon of a vanished nightmare—on the back of its receding coach. (Have been thinking a good deal about spirals lately in connection with my work on space and time).[34]

⊕ Nov. 5, 1964, 7.30 AM   **23.**

End of a dream, but recalled rather long bit (the longest since I started to check): seeing my mother off. Ten minutes to 1 PM— her train leaves at 1 PM. We take a taxi and arrive at four min-utes to one. By now the railway station idea has been dropped and she must walk up to a kind of *téléphérique* station[35] on the

31. Baron George (Yuri) Rausch von Traubenberg (1897–1919) joined as a cavalry officer the volunteer army in the South fighting the Bolsheviks and was killed during an attack. See *Speak, Memory*, 188, 196–200, 203 ("All emotions, all thoughts, were governed in Yuri by one gift: a sense of honor equivalent, morally, to absolute pitch," *Speak, Memory*, 200).

32. The Nabokov country estate south of St. Petersburg.

33. Pnin, keenly conscious of his heart's uncertain condition, "never attempted to sleep on his left side, even in those dismal hours of the night when the insomniac longs for a third side after trying the two he has" (311).

34. This apparently evolved into *Ada*, whose origin and philosophical core is discussed in part 4 of the novel, which takes up the problem of Time in motion.

35. Aerial cable lift.

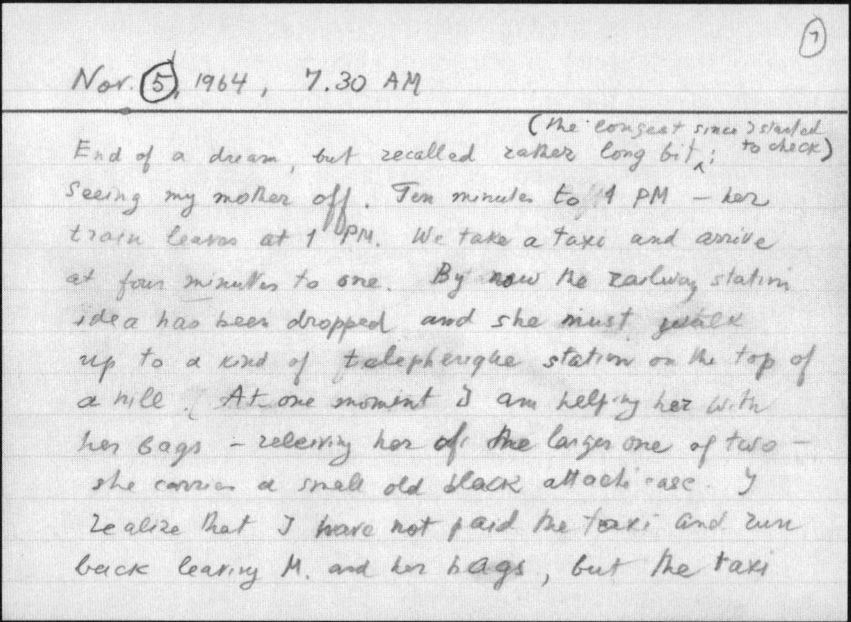

⑦

Nov. ⑤ 1964 , 7.30 AM

(The longest since I started to check)
End of a dream, but recalled rather long bit :
Seeing my mother off. Ten minutes to 1 PM — her
train leaves at 1 PM. We take a taxi and arrive
at four minutes to one. By now the railway station
idea has been dropped and she must get up
up to a kind of téléphérique station on the top of
a hill. At one moment I am helping her with
her bags — relieving her of the larger one of two —
she carries a small old black attaché case. I
realize that I have not paid the taxi and run
back leaving M. and her bags, but the taxi

FIGURE 8. The beginning of the longest record of a dream Nabokov
managed to retain on awakening.

top of a hill. At one moment I am helping her with her bags—
relieving her of the larger one of two—she carries a small old
black attaché-case. I realize that I have not paid the taxi and
run back leaving M. and her bags, but the taxi

<NEW CARD> Nov. 5, cont.

___

has gone. I know, however, that he will presently come back
with another fare—try to figure out how soon—realize it's quite
a way, also realize that his method was to leave the small con-
traption or essential part of it, with running motor—all this
securely attached and locked—I see the gap in the queue and
take one of the empty cars at the taxi stand—a common pro-
cedure in my dream. Meanwhile M. has followed a porter up
the hill to the circular pavilion-like affair at the top. I have not
kissed her goodbye and this bothers me, but as I start hurrying

<NEW CARD> Nov. 5, cont.

___

up the hill I become aware that the entire hill—or island-like
hill—or island-like hill-like liner—is about to move away. I
wonder how more people are not carried away since visitors
are not warned to get off, and now decide to do so at once.
I scramble and slide down a kind of moraine slope feeling
that I am taking a dangerous course on an unusual side of the
hill-island. Still hope to glimpse my mother from some point
before the whole thing moves away. Apparently it is

<NEW CARD> Nov. 5, cont.

___

moving already and I am worried by the possibility of a fissure opening under my feet. I am now above a sheer drop
of rock and there is water below, we are definitely moving,
I must get off, but do not want to get wet. A jutting branch

helps me to swing across the water and drop on the safe side without wetting my feet. I make my way along a scrubby path. Young woman with little boy, older woman presently appears, and they walk towards the landing. (The woman says to her aunt:

<NEW CARD> Nov. 5, cont.

"*Tu sais, il fera si bon dormir bien au chaud là-bas*".[36] The little boy raises some objection but smilingly, and I think he must be sort of bored to be with those two women to whom he is not related—but a polite, good-natured little boy. I now see from the footpath along which they have wandered away the entire—receding—hill-liner with a lot of newcomers and their luggage and cars at the foot of the thing. But I cannot make out my mother among small silhouettes high up in the pavilion.

■ *The beginning of this dream has an antecedent in chapter 3 of* The Real Life of Sebastian Knight: *V. and his mother frantically pacing the platform because they can't board the train, in which to escape the Bolshevik-overrun Russia, without Sebastian, who is nightmare-worthy late: "The thought that in a minute or two the train would move off and that we should have to return to a dark cold attic . . . was utterly disastrous. . . . Eight forty-five, eight-fifty . . ." The train was scheduled to depart at 8:40. Likewise, the second part at once brings to mind the ending of that novel: there, a dying man is fancying ". . . the wrench, the parting, the quay of life gently moving away aflutter with handkerchiefs: ah! He was already on the other side, if he could see the beach receding; no, not quite . . . thus one who has come to see a friend away, may stay on deck too late, but still not become a traveller."*

36. "It will be so nice to sleep well in that warm place, you know."

"The Enchanter" (1939) has a sentence resembling the initial set-
ting of the dream: "He refused tea, explaining that at any moment
the car he had ordered at the station would arrive, that it already
contained his luggage (this detail, as occurs in dreams, had a cer-
tain glimmer of meaning)."

The mention of a téléphérique *lift points in the opposite direction*
in time: in 1975, hunting butterflies in the Alps, Nabokov fell down
a steep slope and lay helpless for some time while cable cars glided
above him at regular intervals, their fares apparently taking an
elderly gentleman, sprawling supine and gesturing for attention,
for a jolly and drunken tourist.

⊕ Nov. 6, 1964 10.30 PM   *24.*

Watching a series entitled *Cinq colonnes à la une* on the French
television programme[37] at around 9.30 PM (did not note the
time and did not stay till the end), saw an island with "pas-
sengers" that broke off the mainland, sailing out into the
ocean—an illustration from a Jules Verne book shown in connection with a village built on water in South America.

Reminded me of the "island-full-liner" dream jotted down
yesterday morning!

Nov. 6, 1964, 8.00 AM—could recall nothing.[38]   *25.*

Nov. 7 — —

End of dream: my mother is upset about something and everything my father says makes it worse. He gives me a bound
volume of the *Illustration* or *Graphic*. I turn the pages, sitting
with legs crossed. My mother on the verge of tears quietly

37. An evening news report program that ran from 1959 to 1968.
38. Recorded retroactively.

leaves the room (we seem to be abroad in a hotel or a villa, my parents are young but I am a grown man). My father follows her. I hear his voice going on and on in the next room. *"Ne descendez pas si vous êtes indispose, et tous seront contents"*[39] (an impossible scene in the real past) I feel dreadfully embarrassed and cannot decide <VERSO> whether to concentrate on the magazine (where there is a chess diagram on the right-side page) so as not to hear what is being said, or shut the heavy volume and go away. He also says something about her wishing only that a street be named after him.

25-A. Nov. 7, 1964 3.00 PM

Slept after lunch, which seldom do. End of vivid dream: V. and I are buying Christmas presents. She warmly greets a young woman who comes in as we are about to go. They chat for a moment and then part. I wonder who she is and reflect that it is probably a "nice nurse" she had at the hospital. I stretch my hand to shake hands with the girl who hesitates clumsily for a moment before taking it. (During our morning walk we had met the small boy of V's hairdresser. He had had an operation—leg—but now walked quite well. She shook hands with him, I did not).

26. Nov. 8, 1964 9.15

Woke up very late. Some kind of party connected with the (real) fact that my nephew V.S. is about to get married.[40] He wants to show me something. We go out: we are now in a

39. "If you are unwell, then don't come down, it will make everybody happy."
40. Vladimir Sikorski, only son of Elena Sikorski, VN's sister (born in 1939 on the same day as VN, April 23), a United Nations interpreter and translator of VN's *Strong Opinions* into French (*Intransigeances*, Paris: Julliard, 1985), married to Nilly Sikorski, née Harounoff, on December 23, 1964.

large field for rifle practice. He gives me something extremely precious to hold, saying "this will interest you," and goes away with his rifle gaily and rather carelessly twirling it: I cry out jokingly that I hope he knows at what end of the field the targets are—my end or his—but he is already far. I examine what he has given me to hold. It is something he <NEW CARD> had to construct for the same competitional purpose as his rifle shooting. It is a butterfly very neatly spread between two leaves of cellophane somehow glued together. The thing can be folded but the fold must not come across the butterfly, which would be fatal. I am terribly afraid to spoil the precious object. The butterfly itself is particularly rare—a remarkable aberration of a ♂ [male] *Plebejus,*[41] with an extensive spread of golden orange over the upper side as in a ♀ [female]. I tell myself that these auroral scales <NEW CARD> are more physical (structural) than chemical (which scientifically is not nonsense). It glistens beautifully in the sun. I decide to fold the object, do so very carefully, but having done so am not sure I have folded it properly. His mother[42] has now appeared and I give her the thing half-afraid she'll open it and perhaps find something is dreadfully wrong.

(On the 6th V. had been asked by my nephew to visit the flat he was arranging for himself and his bride, and yesterday I had been coloring with a yellow crayon the outline figure of a *machaon*).[43]

41. A genus of the *Lycaenidae* family of butterflies, the so-called Blues, in which VN was a recognized expert, having named and described one European species, *Lysandra cormion* Nabokov, 1941 (it later turned out to be a hybrid), to which he dedicated a poem ("A Discovery," 1943) and several Nearctic ones, including the famous protected "Karner Blue," *Plebejus samuelis* Nabokov, 1943.

42. Elena Sikorski (1906–2000), née Nabokov, VN's younger sister.

43. *Papilio machaon* Linnaeus, 1758, a large, brightly colored, spur-winged butterfly commonly known as the swallowtail. It visits three of VN's novels, a short story, and the book of memoirs; there, he recollects the event that started his lifelong entomology passion: in June 1906 on the Vyra estate his "guiding angel [. . .] pointed out [. . .] a rare visitor, a splendid, pale-yellow creature with black blotches, blue

27. Nov. 9, 1964 8.30 AM

Could not recall anything.
End of V's dream:
She is being released from a Portuguese prison with the stipulation that the release has to be repeated four times. She is walking out of the stone gateway, she is barefoot, carrying baby Dm., stepping upon the old St Petersburg type of cobbled pavement. The atmosphere is rather like that of the Inquisition than of Nazism. (We have never been to Portugal, and Dm. is now 30 years of age)

■ *The sentence in parentheses is one of several that seem to point up that Nabokov entertained the idea of publishing selected records from his experiment, perhaps together with some other dreams of his; else it is difficult to explain why he often furnishes information for the benefit of an outside reader: his son's age or the fact that his wife does not smoke (see the last phrase, also in parentheses, in the next record).*

28. Nov. 10, 1964 8.00 AM

Ragged end only: Dm. returns from trip out of town where he had been to a drugstore or barbershop (quite unknown in waking life) and tells V. that they are a little surprised and hurt I have not called for a lotion I had ordered long ago and which—as he says—they have lovingly prepared. I had completely forgotten it and am now annoyed with Dm. that he did not tell me he was going there. In the meantime V. is sitting in the armchair of our living room here, reading and smoking (she does not smoke).

---

crenels, and a cinnabar eyespot above each chrome-rimmed black tail. As it probed the inclined flower from which it hung, its powdery body slightly bent, it kept restlessly jerking its great wings, and my desire for it was one of the most intense I have ever experienced" (*Speak, Memory*, 120).

Nov. 10, 1964 8.00 AM

V's dream: Topazia Markevich[44] tells us that she finds it very difficult to *begin* making the Italian translation of my story ("Lik").[45] V. says she will start for her. T.M. has brought down (from Villars?[46]) Dm.'s car so V. can start right away (!) The hood is open and all one has to do is detach the denture like dark thing along the edge of the car's inner mouth (!) using a *stameska*-like instrument;[47] but one has to be careful because at the very front, where the sides meet, Dm.'s artificial dentures (does not have any) are enclosed in the brown, earthen, curtain-like projections. <VERSO> Now Dm. stands at my elbow warning me to be careful and not to break the plates. I manage to take them out with perfect ease, and the rest of the work (removing the brown things) should be now quite easy for Topazia. Meantime Dm. is quite gay, has his own teeth.

Nov. 11, 1964 6.00 AM Four cards   29.

Woke up early, decided to jot this down though very sleepy. I was thinking the other day about the odd fact that in my "professional" dreams I so very seldom actually compose anything. But to-night, at the end of a dream, I was granted a very nice sample. I am lying on a couch and dictating to V. Apparently I have been dictating from written cards in my hand, but this I dictate in the act of composing it. It refers to a new, expanded *The Gift*. My young man F. <NEW CARD>

44. Topazia Markevitch, née Princess Caetani (1921–1990), ex-wife of Igor Markevitch, a prominent composer and conductor, was the Nabokovs' close acquaintance from neighboring Vevey.
45. A 1938 short story that Nabokov included in a special collection of four select stories (*Nabokov's Quartet*, 1966).
46. A village in canton Vaud, near Montreux.
47. *Stameska* is Russian for a chisel.

is speaking of his destiny, *already accomplished,* and of his having vaguely but constantly known that it was to be a great one. I am saying this slowly in Russian:[48] *«о чем бы я ни думал, от каждой мысли откидывалось как тень, простираясь внутрь меня, мое великое будущее».*[49] I am dictating this very slowly, strongly stressing the *внутрь меня,*[50] weighing every word, hesitating whether to use *великое* or *великолепное,*[51] wondering if *«великое»* did not make the inward extending shadow too long and large, finally settling for that epithet. Simultaneously I am thinking rather <small>NEW CARD</small> smugly that nobody had ever rendered the theme of nostalgia better than I and that I had subtly introduced (in a wholly imaginary passage of *The Gift* in Russian) a certain secret strain: *before* actually anybody had left forever those avenues and fields, a sense of never-returning was already inscribed into them. I am also conscious, while slowly, word by word, dictating "Fyodor's" phrase, that it will please and surprise Vé. because I am generally not good at evolving orally anything out of the ordinary unless I have written it down, <small>NEW CARD</small> and moreover I quite clearly appreciate the fact that this metaphorical shadow of the future cast by every thought in F.'s youth extended *back* into the psyche (instead of lying ahead as it would be more customary for the future to do).

I should note that some twenty-five years ago, in New York,[52] I had been toying with the idea of continuing my *Дар,*[53] i.e. going on to F's & Z's life in Paris.

48. ". . . in Russia" in the original, a slip.
49. "No matter what I was thinking of, every thought cast forth my great future like a shadow, extending inward."
50. Inward, inside of me.
51. Great or magnificent.
52. In 1939 the Nabokovs were still in Paris, sailing to New York in May 1940.
53. The Russian title of what was later translated as *The Gift.*

■ *Nabokov used to dictate his manuscripts to his wife, who would type them up (and often retype more than once, after heavy correction). Dar (The Gift), his last Russian novel, was finished in 1937, published in 1952, in English in 1963. Fyodor Godunov-Cherdyntsev is the main actor and occasional narrator; Zinaida Mertz is his love. A projection of the Russian phrase from this dream runs throughout the novel. The sequel Nabokov mentions has in part survived: it takes the couple to 1939 Paris, where Fyodor is unrecognizably abrasive and even boorish while Zina soon gets run over by a car in an accident reminiscent of Lolita's mother's death.*

Nov. 12, 1964 7.30 AM Could not recall   **30.**

Nov. 13, 1964 6.30 AM   **31.**

Poignant bitter-sweet dream permeated with tenderness and hopelessness. Short girl, rather dumpy, slatternly dressed, bare-necked, face very attractive but not flawlessly pretty, broadish jaws, flattish nose, wonderful complexion, smooth, warmly colored skin, pale-blue eyes, bedraggled fair hair. Am trying in vain to console her: she has been badly hurt by faithless heartless young husband, a shadowy gay-dog figure in the background. I am doing my best to make her understand how dreadfully sorry I am for her, but she is completely wrapped up <NEW CARD> in her taciturn grief, is absolutely impenetrable no matter how I strain to "reach her," «пробиться к ней»,[54] as I tell her in Russian—but all in vain, she looks up at me with apprehensive hunted gaze, ready to stiffen, bothered, resenting my sympathy which is quite genuine but not free from desire. (The young man is—a very obscure feeling—related to me—perhaps Dm.?!)

54. Get through to her.

Oct. 14, 1964 cont.[55]

Later, a "museum" dream, ending in my picking up an autobiographical work by Dobuzhinsky the painter,[56] but here writing about butterfly-collecting. (He had been my teacher of drawing and I had seen him many years later in New York and Vermont). I cannot find the index, but then realize the volume consists of two books bound together and the index comes after the first.

32.   Oct. <sic> 14, 1964, 8.30 AM

Several dreams, one of them keenly erotic, replaying (for perhaps the five-hundredth time) with perfect freshness a fugue of my early youth.

At around 3 AM an abstract, fatidic vision: a death-sign consisting of two roundish golden-yellow blobs with blurred edges, placed not quite side by side but more so than one above the other, for an instant, on my right. The point was that I was supposed to be competing in this specific vision with V.—who would see it first?—but was now too sleepy to check with her and fell asleep again.[57]

55. This is a continuation of the record of the same day. By a curious mistake, VN puts, instead of Nov. 14, the date on which he started his experiment. He continues to write the erroneous "Oct." for the next two days.

56. Mstislav Dobuzhinski (1875–1957), a famous Russian artist. This is another note that seems to be done for the benefit of an outside reader.

57. At the time, Nabokov had as many years to live as his wife would outlive him by. This strange dream, with its curious competition—who would see the death sign first—has an even stranger antecedent in Mandelstam's piercing 1931 poem "Net, ne spriatat'sia mne . . ." [No, I can't hide . . .], addressing his wife: "My s toboiu poedem na 'A' i na 'B', posmotret' kto skoree umret" [You and I will ride tram 'A' and tram 'B,' to see who is to die first]. The Nabokovs read and liked Mandelstam's late poems, published only posthumously, this one in 1961, in the second issue of the Russian almanac *Vozdushnye puti* (Aerial Ways, New York).

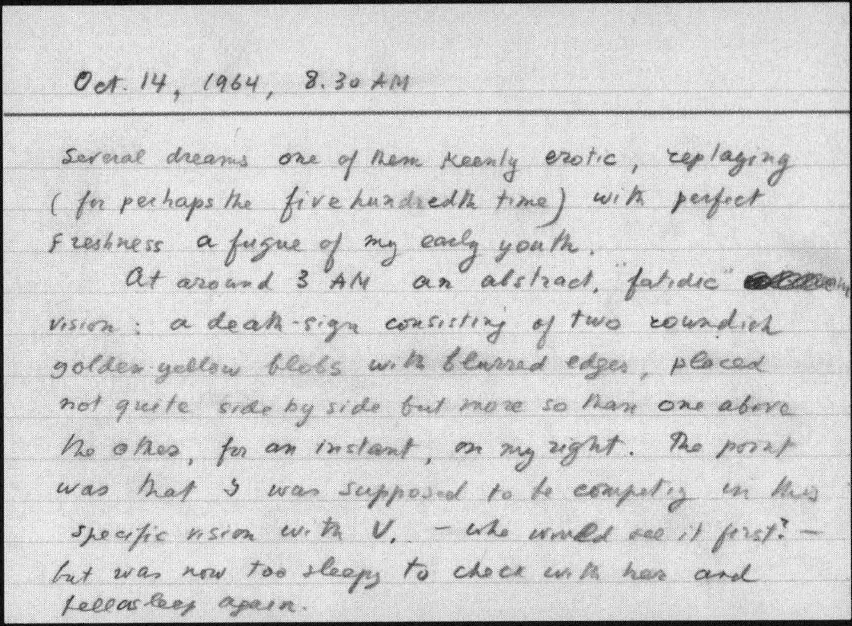

Oct. 14, 1964, 8.30 AM

Several dreams one of them keenly erotic, replaying
(for perhaps the five hundredth time) with perfect
freshness a fugue of my early youth.

    At around 3 AM an abstract, "fatidic" ~~a~~
vision : a death-sign consisting of two roundish
golden-yellow blobs with blurred edges, placed
not quite side by side but more so than one above
the other, for an instant, on my right. The point
was that I was supposed to be competing in this
specific vision with V. — who would see it first? —
but was now too sleepy to check with her and
fell asleep again.

FIGURE 9. For three days Nabokov marked his November records as "October,"
as if restarting the experiment from day one.

33. Oct. <sic> 15, 1964 8.30 AM

Good "artistic" dream.

Am in motel, have just awoken, V. not there (she is spending the night with A. in town),[58] Dm. still asleep in next room. Suddenly I see from window a number of men whom I immediately place as the Red Army performers (singers, dancers) who I know are given <sic> a show in town that night. I tell V. (who is with me after all): Look, the Russians! They are making their way, one after the other, in the wake of a tall fellow with a fishing rod, along a strip of riverside grass and then along another strip at right angles—heading for the rive to fish.[59]

<NEW CARD> Oct. 15, 1964 cont.

All of them in natty uniforms, blue trousers, brown tunics, carrying fishing rods. As they reach the corner of the lawn and are about to turn they do so in a deliberately comic manner, especially a short fellow in very wide pants. They are all humming and softly oozing string-music, and the villagers (Minnesotans or Dakotans) are very much amused and interested. The weather is bleak and rough, with ragged dark grey clouds, a strong wind impedes their progress, it is about to rain, but I realize that for a Russian it is wonderful fishing weather.

34. After a blank spell: could not recall anything yesterday or the day before yesterday.

58. Probably Anna Feigin (1890–1973), VN's wife's cousin. The Nabokovs shared a Berlin apartment with her in 1932–37 and later cared for her in New York and, from 1968, in Montreux.

59. It could be indeed *rive* (French for riverbank), or just "river" missing the ultima.

Nov. 18, 1964 7.30 AM

Several nasty dreams & dreamlets:

Leaving the stranger, a Russian or Spanish general to his tea, I slipped into the next room: I knew he was dangerous—a ruthless agent. I tried to bolt the door, fumbled at the latch, it was hard to push in. Suddenly I collected my wits, I told myself it was shameful to fear that man. I decided to go back and as I re-entered the living room I stepped into a blast of blackness.

In another dream I had to prepare a lecture consisting of four parts or rather

<NEW CARD> Nov. 18, 1964 cont.

answers to questions (confusion with remembered exams of my own student days) and had only ten minutes (it was 8.50 AM) to finish the thing before my lecture began. I knew the subject very vaguely and what I had written down was illegible.

In a third dream I had got out of bed and realized that in addition to some basic dreary old illness I had developed suddenly a deep case of bronchitis.[60]

Nov. 19, 1964 8.00 AM   *35.*

Several fast-fading dreams. In one, I learned that Paulhan[61] had died of a stroke; in another somebody discussed "antisemitism in the world of waiters."

60. Thirteen years later, bronchitis will be an immediate cause of his death. On March 19, 1977, his last year, Nabokov jots down in his agenda book: "Beginning of anoth. bout with бронchitis" (*sic*: a Russian-English hybrid).

61. Jean Paulhan (1884–1968), French writer and publisher whom Nabokov met in Paris in 1932.

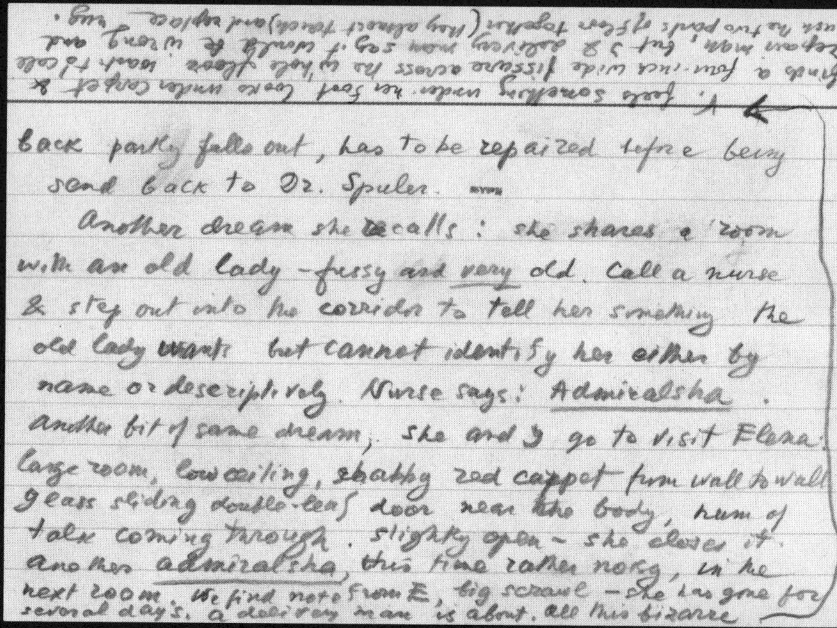

back partly falls out, has to be repaired before being sent back to Dr. Spuler.

Another dream she recalls: she shares a 'room with an old lady — fussy and very old. Call a nurse & step out into the corridor to tell her something the old lady wants but cannot identify her either by name or descriptively. Nurse says: Admiralsha. Another bit of same dream, she and I go to visit Elena: large room, low ceiling, shabby red carpet from wall to wall, glass sliding double-leaf door near the body, hum of talk coming through. slightly open — she closes it. Another admiralsha, this time rather noisy, in the next room. We find note from E, big scrawl — she has gone for several days. a delivery man is about. all this bizarre

FIGURE 10. One of Nabokov's wife's dreams recorded.

V. dreamt that we have on our table an object resembling a travelling-clock made of a square piece of wood with a small dial in the middle but only one figure. Suddenly somebody (another doctor?) tells us that this is Dr. Spuler's diploma: that he has just passed his Ph.D. (sic!).[62] We wonder why it is there and decide to send it to him. Somebody drops it—the <VERSO> back partly falls out, has to be repaired before being sent back to Dr. Spuler.

Another dream she recalls: she shares a room with an old lady—fussy and *very* old. Call a nurse & step out into the corridor to tell her something the old lady wants but cannot identify her either by name or descriptively. Nurse says: *admiralsha.*[63]

Another bit of same dream; she and I go to visit Elena: large room, low ceiling, shabby red carpet from wall to wall, glass sliding double-leaf door near the body, hum of talk coming through.[64] Slightly open—she closes it. Another *Admiralsha*, this time rather noisy, in the next room. We find note from E., big scrawl—she has gone for several days. A delivery man is about. All this bizarre. V. feels something under her foot, looks under carpet & finds a four-inch wide fissure across the whole floor, wants to call repairman, but I & delivery man say it would be wrong and push the two parts of floor together (they almost touch) and replace rug.

Nov. 20, 1964 8.30 AM   36.

Walking in town (anonymous), notice that am on asphalt, empty, between barricades. There is shooting all around. A helmeted man in blue yells at me to take cover. I

62. Dr. Spuhler was the Nabokovs' Swiss physician through the 1970s. VN spells his name correctly in his diaries of later years.

63. Wife of an admiral, in informal Russian.

64. VN's sister (see p. 63, note 42), who lived in Geneva.

ponder—should I listen to him? However, I do—I jump into a kind of excavation. One of several dreams.

Compare to Véra's second dream under same date!

Nov. 20, 1964, 9.00 AM

V's dream, first one. At station or port we go to meet the Ustinovs.[65] Only Suzanne is clear: she is the star, she is *"entourée"*<,> children in background. New governess with her young man, a pimp who thinks that I am interested in his lady, and nudges Véra cockily. Before a fight can develop Véra says: come, come he is married. Present in her mind is the girl they had before with *her* "pimp" who also etc. (an old story). Suzanne has many dogs with her and suddenly everything is held up—one of them, a large poodle, raises his hind-leg in <VERSO> the middle of the stage. Also two small poodle pups, one grey, one black, Véra takes up and carries the grey which at first is nervous, but then surrenders. We go into large building with a helpful concierge. Lots of people want to take the lift which goes up & down below our level. In the lift V. realizes that the dog in her arms has been replaced by a still smaller black one. Search for the grey. The concierge thinks it might be in the flat of Lord Torno (or Tornu) a newspaper magnate recently knighted. We go there. Maid, lord. He finally returns the dog. It welcomes V. ecstatically though had been grumpy before.

Nov. 20, 1964 9.00 AM   Compare to my dream same night!

Second dream, Véra's: we see from our high floor window revolutionary crowds coming in trucks who begin: (1) playing soccer on a field beyond the road, and (2) digging a wide

---

65. Peter Ustinov (1921–2004), English actor and the Nabokovs' neighbor and acquaintance. Suzanne Ustinov, née Cloutier, his second wife (from 1954 to 1971).

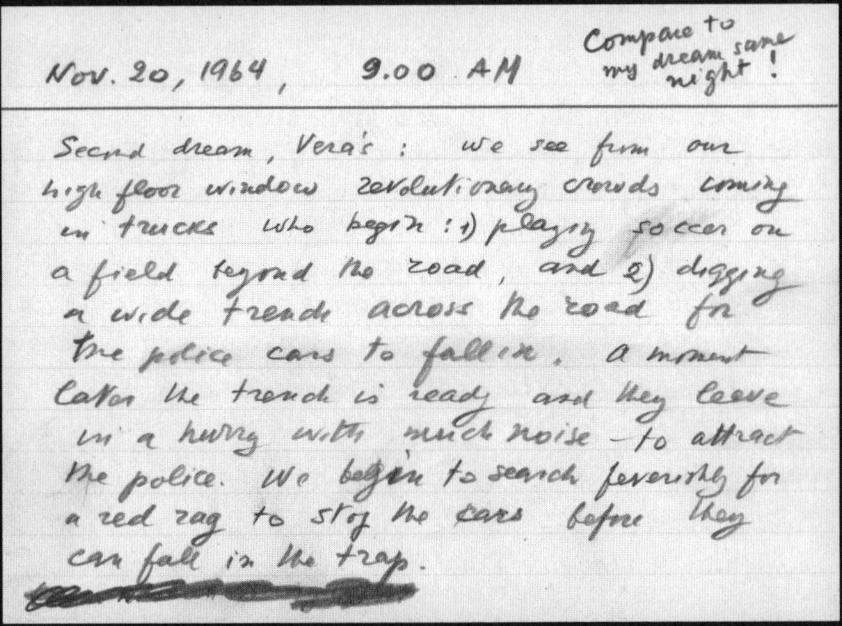

Nov. 20, 1964, 9.00 AM *Compare to my dream same night!*

Second dream, Vera's : we see from our high floor window revolutionary crowds coming in trucks who begin : 1) playing soccer on a field beyond the road, and 2) digging a wide trench across the road for the police cars to fall in. A moment later the trench is ready and they leave in a hurry with much noise — to attract the police. We begin to search feverishly for a red rag to stop the cars before they can fall in the trap.

FIGURE 11. His wife had a dream akin to his own the night before.

trench across the road for the police cars to fall in. A moment later the trench is ready and they leave in a hurry with much noise—to attract the police. We begin to search feverishly for a red rag to stop the cars before they can fall in the trap.

37.   Nov. 21, 1964 8.30 AM

Véra's dream: we're in Denmark, on a tour of the country, with motocycle <*sic*> & sidecar to be driven by a young Danish woman slightly recalling Filippa.[66] Sometimes I am outside and somebody, sister or Dm., also is inside with V. in this hybridish car, Véra being in the left corner. The Danish girl arrives with a black suitcase at the last moment and sits in the sidecar. Two trucks (one parked)—we pass between. We reach a narrow river, we stop at the bank, unlawfully, and I cross toward the hills on a private quest. Danish girl follows me and V. is left with small Dm. and vehicle. V. rather complicatedly <*sic*> removes the car with girl (who has run back) to path going up through <NEW CARD> (cont.) small cafe. As we come back we find a man who rocks <?> his chair to block the path and is reading a book, leg<s> cross<ed>. We squeeze through. He becomes abusive. Véra says: "you are not a European (meaning he might be a German from the colonies), I dont know *what* you are"—and then it dawns upon her that he is simply a rude Dane at home resentful of foreigners.

38.   22 Nov. 1964 3.15 AM

In a kind of lecture-hall during an informal performance or rehearsal of lecture. On the platform my father seated at a small table is reading and discussing something. Several

66. Anna Filippa Rolf (1924–1978), Swedish poet, Nabokov's admirer and translator into Swedish. The admiration of this high-strung woman grew burdensome for the Nabokovs—see Stacy Schiff, *Véra (Mrs. Vladimir Nabokov)*, 272–87, 326–29.

people between the stage and me. Am eagerly taking down
what he says. My mother is among the four or five people sitting in front of me. My father is now elucidating a point. I see
and appreciate it and clear my throat a trifle too loudly while
trying to jot down his argument as fully as possible. From the
stage he suddenly addresses me—I nod my head supposing
he is making the possible objection I have foreseen; but instead, he says to me: "Even if you are <NEW CARD> bored you
might have the decency to sit quietly." I feel deeply injured
and reply (textual words [transl. from Russian], chosen and
uttered with great care and dignity): "I think your observation to me is most unjust. I was listening attentively and
with enormous interest." I get up and start to leave hoping I
shall be called back. But I hear behind me my father's voice
resuming his speech with a little less force than before. I vi-
sualize in a medallion of light to-morrow morning's interview
with him—imagine him in his beige dressing—<NEW CARD>
gown. Shall I ignore what happened? Will he refer to it? I
decide philosophically—a similar case has come up before
within dream experience—that time will decide (curious that
I saw myself imagining the future in my dream and vaguely
recalling a past and that a sense of future, of time, clearly
though somewhat crudely existed in my mind, i.e. I distinctly
perceived the degree of difference in comparative reality between the dream vision and the dream prevision). It is odd
that my father who was so good-natured, and gay, is always
so morose and grim in my dreams.

■ *VN's father was killed in a lecture-hall of sorts (the Berlin Phil-
harmonic Hall, used for public lectures) in March 1922 by a bullet
intended for another man, Pavel Miliukov, a prominent left-wing
member of the Russian liberal party of which V. D. Nabokov was a
(moderate) founding member. Cf. the earlier Dream III, also a later
one, Dream X, in part 3. Cf. also:*

"His father often appeared to him in dreams, as if just returned from some monstrous penal servitude, having experienced physical tortures which it was forbidden to mention, now changed into clean linen—it was impossible to think of the body underneath—and with a completely uncharacteristic expression of unpleasant, momentous sullenness, with a sweaty brow and slightly bared teeth, sitting at table in the circle of his hushed family. But when, overcoming his sensation of the spuriousness of the very style foisted on fate, he nevertheless forced himself to imagine the arrival of a live father, aged but undoubtedly his, and the most complete, most convincing possible explanation of his silent absence, he was seized, not by happiness, but by a sickening terror—which, however, immediately disappeared and yielded to a feeling of satisfied harmony when he removed this meeting beyond the boundary of earthly life." (The Gift, *99–100)*

In his lectures The Borders of Gnoseology, *Florensky calls this phenomenon paramnesia: "There is, strictly speaking, memory of the future just as there is memory of the past, both having to do with the proceeding order of time but shifting the past and the future, along with their temporal characteristics, to the present" (Florensky 1996, 56–57).*

39. 23 Nov. 1964 6.45 AM

End of a long "butterfly" dream which started after I had fallen asleep following upon a sterile awakening at 6.15 AM. Have arrived (by funiculaire?) to a collecting ground at timberland (in Switzerland? in Spain?), but in order to get to it have to cross the hall of a large gay hotel. Very spry and thin, dressed in white, skip down the steps on the other side and find myself on the marshy border of a lake. Lots of bog flowers, rich soil, colorful, sunny, but not one single butterfly (familiar sensation in dream). Instead of a net am carrying a huge spoon [see next]

—cannot understand how I managed to forget my net and bring this thing—wonder how I shall catch anything with it. Notice a kind of letter box open on the right side, full of butterflies somebody has collected and left there. One is alive—a marvellous aberration of the Green fritillary with unusually elongated wings, the green all fused together and the brown of an extraordinary variegated hue. It eyes me in conscious agony as I try to kill it by pinching its thick thorax—very tenacious of life. Finally slip it into

<NEW CARD> 23 Nov., cont.

a Morocco case—old, red, zippered. Then realize that all the time a man camouflaged in some way is seated next to me to the left in front of the receptacle in which the butterflies are; and prepares a slide for the microscope. We converse in English. He is the owner of the butterflies. I am very much embarrassed. Offer to return the fritillary. He declines with polite half-heartedness.

■ *When Dmitri Nabokov later described the falling episode, he mentioned that his father "was subsequently reprimanded by the [Davos] hotel staff for stumbling back into the lobby, supported by two bellhops, with his shorts in disarray."*[67]

■ *Verso has a sketched (diagrammed) idea for a chess problem, crossed out. It is very cursorily drawn and lacks the white king; what can be made out seems to form the following position:*

White: K??, Qb7, Rf8, Ne2.
Black: Kd5, Rc5, Rd4, Nc6, pawns c3, d3, e4, e5.

67. *The Original of Laura*, xi.

40.   Nov. 24, 1964 9.00 AM

Very end of dream: dining here in the restaurant downstairs.[68] My nephew, to the right of me, tastes the chicken on his plate and complains to the waiter that it tastes exactly like candle grease.[69] I confirm this.

Nov. 24, 1964 9.00 AM

Véra's dream. Going in two cars to railway station. Ustinovs in first car, we in the second. Policeman stops us and takes us to some kind of establishment. Eventually she and Dm. are sitting on a bench in a snowy park. He says: let us take that car—a kind of open van. He gets in and a man comes up and pulls the car (sic!) to start it rolling. V. is supposed to sit behind but it is waist-full of sand. They get out and the man pushes it back to the curb, saying he's doing it the third time. She says: OK, I'll just take my muff out. She does and next moment she and Dm. are riding along in the car. They go to the police-station to return the car <VERSO> Dm. objects, V. says: ok I'll return the muff. Next moment in room with a policeman who pesters Dm. for something. She says: give the policeman five francs and then: give them to me (being afraid Dm. will be arrested for bribing). She hands it to a grateful policeman.

41.   Nov. 25 & 26, 1964 Forenoon

Did not jot down dreams immediately because too trivial but oddly enough remember both quite clearly. Last night dreamt that got off a transatlantic liner to stroll about a bit—was a few miles from my destination—a tennis club

68. That is, in Montreux Palace Hotel.
69. Vladimir Sikorski (see p. 62, note 40).

where I was to take part in a match but suddenly noticed the white stack of the ship was smoking and moving away;[70] and to-night dreamt I was in a railway coach (American) and a voice on the radio was giving a little talk about me in French. Presently the speaker came across to us and we chatted.

27 Nov. 7.30 AM   42.

Bits of four dreams:

1. Have come home, find Dm. unexpectedly arrived from Milan, at the same time V.'s voice comes gaily from bedroom. Find her lying in bed with books. On floor near bed a basin—a washstand basin—almost full of brown bile. The doctor has been already called.

2. Am reading my father's diary. He writes that he roared with laughter upon finding the minutes of medium-istic séances on the kitchen table (our cook Nikolay Andreevich <NEW CARD> was indeed a spiritist).[71] The cook's papers and various vague objects are displayed before me.

3. In a big bathroom, in an (Italian?) hotel, cannot get to the toilet because [of] hole in ceiling, excrements have fallen into tub. I rush to another toilet in another part of our apartment, but Dm. is there—catches the door I'm opening. Dash down to a third in the corridor.

---

70. Cf. the ending of *Speak, Memory*: ". . . it was most satisfying to make out among the jumbled angles of roofs and walls a splendid ship's funnel, showing from behind the clothesline as something in a scrambled picture—Find What the Sailor Has Hidden—that the finder cannot unsee once it has been seen."

71. The fellow was not, apparently, alien to a form of materialism as well: after the coup d'état of October 1917 and subsequent fleeing of the Nabokovs, their cook appropriated some items belonging to his former masters, among them a photograph picture album that surfaced, minus the silver plating on the covers, in the 1970s.

A maid is there cleaning up—tells me that Chaykovski
the composer is too ill with cancer to be operated.
4. Am writing down a colorful dream—which on waking
up I cannot recall!

27 Nov., 1964 8.00 AM

Some points in those dreams were taken up by reality without
delay! Among the letters in the mail this morning was a blurb
sent for approval by my London publisher of EO[72] in which
I cannot approve a conspicuous reference to Chaykovski's
opera. Another correspondent sends me the galley proof [of]
my father's prison diary. And V. complains she feels a pain in
her vesicle and suggests cancelling the marcassin Mme C. is
about to buy.[73]

Three sterile nights in a row!

73. Nov. 30, 1964 4.00 AM

End of muddled dream—an exhibition of Spanish cars which
was also an exhibition of specimens of a (unknown) Sierra
Nevada race of *Parnassius mnemosyne*.[74] In the far vista of the
dream two men in overalls were holding and hoisting a whitish gate-like affair.

5.30 AM

Verbal dream. I frequently dream of extraordinarily elaborate—
sometimes even international—rhyme words. In the present

72. *Eugene Onegin*, which VN translated and supplied with a thousand pages of
copious commentary, was brought out in Great Britain in late 1964 by Routledge
& Kegan Paul.

73. Jacqueline Callier, the Nabokovs' secretary and typist in Montreux who continued for many years to assist Véra Nabokov after VN's death.

74. Clouded Apollo, a beautiful swallowtail butterfly, appearing in the pages of
many of VN's writings, esp. in *The Gift* and *Ada*.

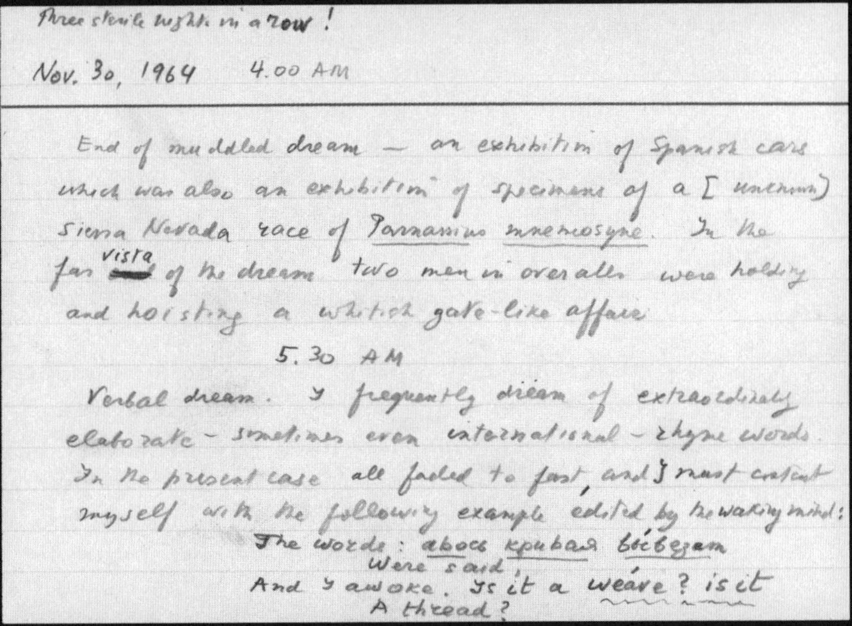

Three sterile nights in a row !

Nov. 30, 1964   4.00 AM

End of muddled dream — an exhibition of Spanish cars which was also an exhibition of specimens of a [unknown) Sierra Nevada race of Parnassius mnemosyne. In the far vista of the dream two men in overalls were holding and hoisting a whitish gate-like affair

5.30 AM

Verbal dream. I frequently dream of extraordinarily elaborate - sometimes even international - rhyme words. In the present case all faded too fast, and I must content myself with the following example edited by the waking mind:

The words: above кривая вбежала
Were said.
And I awoke. Is it a weave? is it
A thread?

FIGURE 12. "Three sterile nights in a row!" at the top records a gap in recording, when Nabokov could not recollect his dreams directly after the odd month confusion (see fig. 9).

case all faded too fast and I must content myself with the
following example edited by the waking mind:

The words: *авось кривая вывезет*
Were said,
And I awoke. Is it a weave? is it
A thread?[75]

44.   Dec. 2, 1964 8.15 AM

Véra's dream: Wild West frontier. The landlady of our
rooming place is a cosy old soul resembling the owner of
"Rodnoy" (thirty years ago)[76] but at the same time it is M.
Bourguer (*papeterie* here).[77] Glass rotating door in the hall.
Alsatian in it, one quarter out, patiently waiting to get out.
She lets him out in passing and he at once becomes our
dog. Dish of food for him appears in her hand—carrots etc.
Problem: is he a vegetarian? He is given the food when we
come home.

New instalment: she has bought some stuff for a jumper,
Lena[78] likes it very much, V. suggests she buy what <VERSO>
is left of it at shop. It is somehow illogical, and V. knows it in
her dream—that she cannot buy the same stuff for a skirt yet
there is enough of it to give this advice to her sister. We both
look for the trade mark on the edge to establish if this fabric
is a "teetotaller tissue" <*sic*> or not.

---

75. The Russian saying goes *kuda krivaia vyvezet*, lit. "wherever the curved road
will take"—to rely on the off-chance. The colloquial *avos'* adds to the haphazardness.
The verb *vyvezet*, with its stress on the first syllable, makes a rich English compound
rhyme here.

76. The Nabokovs stayed at pension "Rodnoy" in Fréjus, the French Riviera, in
the summer of 1939.

77. Stationer's shop.

78. Princess Elena Massalsky (1900–1975), née Slonim, Véra Nabokov's older
sister.

Dec. 3, 1964, 8.00 AM   45.

Vague tender erotic dream in a curiously stylized landscape
with pale trees.

Then the end of another: V. and I sitting at a table with a
small garage-man at one end. He is mapping out Dm.'s ca-
reers. It consists of four parts and one of these is in the margin of the sheet of paper which has to be turned clockwise—it
is spread on the deal table.

Dec. 4, 1964, 8.00 AM   46.

Am coming down steps of Lausanne-like railway station and
meet Edmund Wilson.[79] He is about to catch a train. I tell him
I'll go "upstairs" to see him off. He says: only Russians use
"upstairs" in that sense. He walks briskly along the platform
and I notice how fit he looks in a dark-grey suit. We lose each
other in the crowd and the train glides away. I leave the station. I am carrying V's mink coat. Cannot find a taxi.[80] Very
muddy. Have I lost her scarf? No, in the sleeve of the coat.

Dec. 5, 1964, 12.00 PM   47.

Tested memory by writing dream down at least 18 hours after
I had had it. As clear as it was at 7.00 AM. Came back from
somewhere. Had trouble in finding my room in building resembling Goldwyn Hall, Cornell. Met my cousin S. on the
stairs, she had also come to that reunion—whatever it was—
with all her family.[81] They had their rooms where mine ought

79. VN and Wilson (1895–1972), prominent American man of letters, were close
friends from the early 1940s to the late 1950s, drifting apart in later years.
80. Cf. "For some reason, taxis, as in a bad dream, were unobtainable" (*Look at
the Harlequins!*, 4).
81. Sophia ("Onya") Fasolt (1899–1982), née Nabokov, daughter of VN's uncle
Dmitri. She is mentioned in *Speak, Memory*, 26. The 1920 group picture, with VN in
the back row, is of her wedding.

to be. She looked singularly young and I could not quite decide if she was she or her daughter—or granddaughter.[82] Finally I remember that my room was on the third floor but when I got there the corridor was full of garbage, servants were cleaning it up after the Officers Ball.

■ *Dunne insists that the effect of recognizing a daytime event in the preceding dream "escapes attention because observation must be directed precisely and definitely, and the dreams recorded at once."*

48. Dec. 6, 1964, 8.00 AM

Fatidic-sign dream. Awoke with a pang. An abstract, terrible, accident slices apart our life's monogram, instantly separating us. A nightmare blazon, Vé. and VN with profiles in opposite directions.
    C'était le marcassin, probably.[83]

Dec. 6, 1964, 8.30 AM

Véra's dream: a huge gray-stone old fashioned ornate hotel. We have looked over one or two and now this is the third. They stand in water, a kind of granite Venice. Passages full of cabinets, galleries, balconies. From time to time big caterpillars, white with black faces, naked, crawl over the furniture. We reach at the end of a passage a great vestibule. The staff ring a bell every time they notice a caterpillar. I go away to look up a friend. V. notices <VERSO> a long larva crawling along the top of a chest of drawers.

---

82. Marina Ledkovski (1924–2014), née Fasolt, professor of Russian at Barnard College, New York, and Tatiana Selivonik, née Ledkovski (b. 1949), respectively.

83. The wine mentioned in Dream 42. The monogram of their names, forming as it does a "double V," is strangely reproduced, both in French and in Russian, in the name of the place where both of them were to be cremated, fourteen years apart (Vevey).

Another bit of dream: Elena Bromberg[84] has sent a trunk-ful of clothes for Dm. and, with Anuta, Véra is looking them over, wondering how they can fit since he is bigger than everybody; but A. says it will be all right.

In a third bit, Dm. has to sing in a performance. V. finds herself in garden with several rooms. In one of them a girl resembling Petula Clark[85] is singing, loudly, to be noticed, but badly. Dm. says he also lost his part—his "permit" had expired. V. energetically tries to get him <to> extend it.

Dec. 8, 1964 9.00 AM   **49.**

Having tea with friends (Karpoviches?)[86] on lawn before their house. In a deck chair reclining, very old, sick looking, & sweaty, Leo Tolstoy. I wonder if "Karpovich" knows I dont know him or thinks I would not care to know him. I hear him saying to "Karpovich" in vehement Russian: "I do not like his 'Lolita,' but how well he describes the Russian landscape!" Silly.

Dec. 13, 1964 8.30 AM   **50.**

Skipped four nights
   (Did not take down the banal dreams I had lately).
Intensely erotic dream. Blood on sheet.
End of dream: my sister O.,[87] strangely young and languorous. Then V. tells me I must not forget to go to the ocu-

---

84. Anna ("Anuta") Feigin's second cousin (see p. 70, note 58).

85. A popular English songstress (b. 1932), professionally singing since age seven, a star at eleven.

86. Mikhail Karpovich (1888–1959), professor of history at Harvard and publisher of the main Russian literary magazine in America, *The New Review*, and his wife, Tatiana Karpovich (1897–1973), née Potapov. At their country estate near West Wardsboro, Vermont, the Nabokovs spent their first summer in America in 1940 (and then again in 1942).

87. Olga Petkevich (1903–1978), née Nabokov.

list. I find his street but cannot remember the house number. Am agonizingly searching in the telephone book but do not recall his name and, moreover, do not know how to dial the vague number I have in mind—something ending in 492. Then stand near a window, sighing, half-seeing view, brooding over the possible consequence of incest.

■ *This reminds the Nabokov reader—but not Nabokov—of a critical episode at the end of his 1941 novel,* The Real Life of Sebastian Knight, *with its nightmarishly urgent steeple-chase in pursuit of the narrator's half-brother: "I went to the telephone. < . . . > I thumbed the soft greasy book, looking for Dr Starov's number < . . . > ah, there it was: Jasmin 61–93. < . . . > I performed some dreadful manipulations and forgot the number in the middle, and struggled again with the book, and re-dialed, and listened for a while to an ominous buzzing. < . . . > My nerves were on edge" (*LOA, 153*).

Abano[88]

51. Dec. 26, 1964 7.00 AM

Nina Berberov[89] in black open-necked dress was arranging to take me to a distant suburb to fetch Georges Chklaver[90] who was to have dinner with V. and me at our place— wherever that was. I tell V. that I knew very well we had planned to meet Chkl. half-way but N.B. had overruled me. However, V. said, it's OK, we owe him that much (which we don't). I have never seen these people in dream, and it is perhaps worthwhile to jot this down after a considerable interval.

88. Abano Terme, near Padua.
89. Nina Berberov (1901–1993), a writer and former wife of poet Vladislav Khodasevich (1886–1939), Nabokov's friend.
90. Georges Chklaver, or Georgy Shklyaver (1897–1970), professor of law at the University of Paris, VN's acquaintance.

■ *Dunne advises to be on the alert for the time-reversal effect par-*
ticularly on nights preceding a journey or some other expected break
in the routine humdrum, but by this time Nabokov seems tired of
the experiment, his attention dulled, and in any event he must have
forgotten this tip.

28 Dec. 1964 7.00 AM   5**2**.

On second night here (Hotel Due Torri with large coniferous
garden)[91] in doomful half-dream saw the scattered streaks
of dim light between the slats of the shutters as a passage
which I could not identify translated into French (have been
strenuously checking during the last week, in Montreux,
Coindreau's French translation of *Pale Fire*).[92] That was on
the night of 26–27. This night another much more sustained
doomful dream: a tremendous very black larch paradoxically
posing as a

<NEW CARD> Dec. 28, 1964, cont.

Christmas tree completely stripped of its toys, tinsel, and
lights, appeared in its abstract starkness as the emblem of
permanent dissolution. There was nothing but this bleak tree
which was not even a homely fir. (was bothered again by the
lights through the slats and, probably, echoes of my own
lines on various trees—the *if*, & the hickory, in *Pale Fire*;[93]
moreover: a few days ago, on the 23rd, while coming back in
a taxi from Geneva to Montreux after my nephew's wedding
party I said about a festively lit tree near a villa, *ce n'est pas*

91. A five-star hotel in Abano Terme, with thermal pools, etc.
92. *Feu pâle*, trans. R. Girard et M.-E. Coindreau (Paris: Gallimard, 1965).
93. *L'if*, French for the yew-tree. In that novel, both trees are part of the main
theme of death and its aftermath, the first, as an Anglo-French pun (see Ode 3 of
Shade's poem "Pale Fire"), the second, as a familiar memento mori.

même un sapin—c'est un mélèze; but the chauffeur said *non, c'est bien un sapin*).[94]

53. Dec. 29, 1964 7.30 AM

Many dreams more or less forgotten:
Clear end of one: am correcting, with other people, students' examination papers. Of the three I get, the first read proves to be a little masterpiece. The name of the student is Mostel (not known in waking life)*. I am wondering what to give him, an A or an A+. Cannot find my pencil and am, moreover, upset by a sordid and complicated love affair with another's wife (unknown in waking life and not shown in dream). A colleague (I have never in my life corrected

* (V. says there is a famous American actor of that name).[95]

<NEW CARD> Dec. 29, 1964 cont.

papers collectively!) urges me to finish my batch. I still can't find an implement to write with and furthermore am badgered and hampered in my movements by the betrayed husband, a very small man who works with his arms as he pours out a torrent of complaints. In exasperation I take him and send him flying and spinning into a revolving door where he continues to twist at some distance from the ground, in a horizontal position, before falling. Awkward suspense: is he dead? No, he picks himself up and staggers away. We return to the exam. papers.

94. "This is not really a fir-tree—that's a larch" < . . . > "No, this is a fir all right." The point related to VN's dream here is that *un sapin* may colloquially stand for coffin: *sentir déjà le sapin* means to sense one's end approaching, have one foot in the grave.

95. Samuel "Zero" Mostel (1915–1977), a comedian, survived Nabokov by two months.

Dreamt of Cyr. first time since his death in April.[96] Very young—about 15—, slim, handsome, rosy-cheeked, extremely attractive but not too cheerful, at some picnic in the woods (near Praha?[97]); he takes bottles out of a hamper.

Again bothered by lights, this time a large patch on the wall next to my bed (V. says she managed to close *her* shutters completely, I did not in my room). Half-waking, am told that the patch is now higher because it is the badge or <coat of> arms of some nation or other and they were displeased that it was lower than the head of my bed—so hitched it up. A fussy light, with fate and farce merging.

Dec. 30, 1964, 7.30 AM   54.

Have been apparently sunbathing but then dressed and fallen asleep. Woke up not in the usual pinegrove but where there is a path going up diagonally (brief vision of girl in blue dashing up on a bicycle "as she alway [*sic*] does"[98] but in a kind of small hollow, sandy and dingy, right beside the

---

96. Kirill (Cyril) Nabokov (1911–1964), VN's youngest brother.

97. After V. D. Nabokov was killed in Berlin in 1922, Kirill Nabokov lived in Prague with his mother and two sisters, where VN visited them several times before World War II.

98. The source of the phrase within the quotation marks is obscure. It is remotely possible that it was lifted from Edmund Clerihew Bentley's famous detective novel *Trent's Last Case* (1913). The spot has remarkably to do with being roused from sleep early and crudely, as the heroine's husband was found murdered: "I never woke until my maid brought my tea in the morning at seven o'clock. She closed the door leading to my husband's room as she alway did, and I supposed him to be still there. . . . He sometimes slept until quite late in the morning." This book was convolved with Francis Iles's *Before the Fact* and A. Mason's *The House of the Arrow* (see p. 37, note 8) under the title *Three Famous Murder Novels*, selected and exquisitely introduced by Bennett A. Cerf, editor of the Modern Library, and published by Random House in 1941, and it is not improbable that this was the edition that VN read.

highway (on my left). Am dressed in pale green pyjama top (unfamiliar) and dark pants, barefooted, cold feet, looking for my socks. Soviet delegates pass along the road. Then, out of the woods comes a woman and a child, Russians. She tells

<NEW CARD> Dec. 30, 1964, cont.

---

me: I know very well your great friend Mrs Shifrin-Panskaya (never heard of her).[99] I reply perhaps V. has met her, don't remember. The little boy, of 6 or 7, very rosy and bright-eyed and dirty with pinewood sand, vaguely Dm. as a child with a streak of Alexander, N.'s boy, says he's sleepy. Does he take a bath before going to bed? No, no more baths, but a lot of Molière here (tapping his forehead).

Abano
55. Jan. 3, 1965[100]

Philippa Rolf who came here to see us, told us that Nina Berberov had exhibited a letter I had written her (thirty years ago) at the Yale Library.[101] Does not connect very sharply with dream of Dec. 26, 1964, except that I never hear anything about that lady.[102]

99. In his letter of Feb. 2, 1936, from Paris (*Letters to Véra*, 243), VN mentions an émigré cinematic studio manager Semyon Shifrin (1894–1985) who was recommended to him as a possible producer for a film script he was drafting, under the title *Hôtel Magique*—especially curious, given that VN saw that dream in a grand hotel at an Italian spa, with bothersome shafts of light penetrating through the closed slats of the window blinds. In the *TLS* publication, I misspelled the name as "Shigrin," following the misreading in *Transcription*.

100. The experiment ends two days before Véra Nabokov's birthday (January 5).

101. See p. 76, note 66. Nabokov spelled her Christian name (Filippa) variously.

102. Their postwar relationship grew cold.

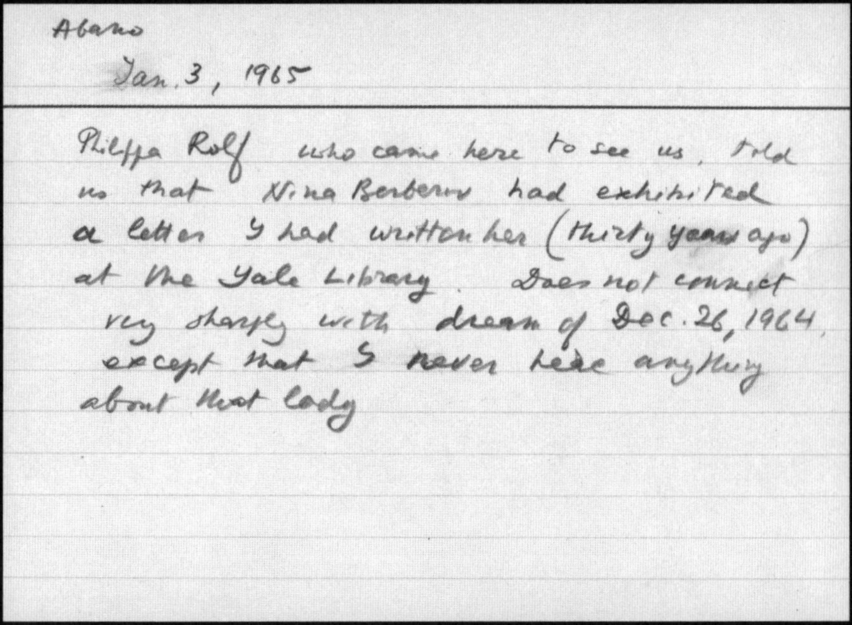

Abano

Jan. 3, 1965

Philippa Rolf who came here to see us, told
us that Nina Berberova had exhibited
a letter I had written her (thirty years ago)
at the Yale Library. Does not connect
very sharply with dream of Dec. 26, 1964,
except that I never hear anything
about that lady

FIGURE 13. The end of the experiment.

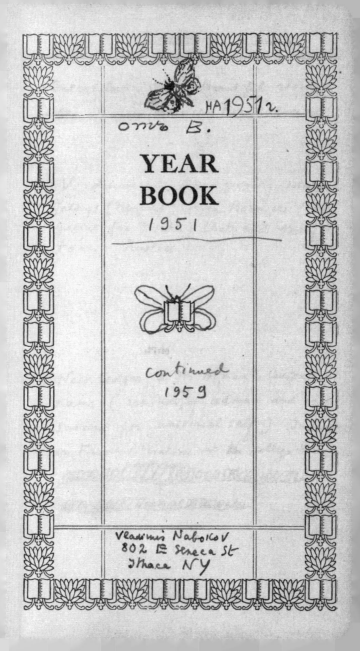

HA1951г.

onto B.

YEAR
BOOK

1951

continued
1959

Vladimir Nabokov
802 E Seneca St
Ithaca NY

PART 3

MORE DREAMS

WHAT FOLLOWS IS a selection of Nabokov's dream records before and after the 1964 experiment, culled, with one exception, from his 1951–59 notebook and from his pocket diaries. Even before he read Dunne's book, Nabokov followed the basic parameters and conditions of *An Experiment with Time*, writing down a dream soon upon awakening, in great detail, without an attempt to interpret it in wake-life terms.

As mentioned in part 1, the manuscripts in his letters and diaries almost always bear signs of Nabokov's intention to prepare some of the dreams for publication: edited words, later insertions, corrected brackets within parentheses, spelled-out numbers, facts known to him but not to an outsider, and so on.

The tiny pages of his yearly leather-bound agenda books are covered with Nabokov's clear, rounded writing in both English and Russian, although his hand becomes very shaky toward the end. The pocket inside the cover kept a standard set of reminder strips to be pasted under the respective date (*"aujourd'hui, c'est l'anniversaire de ma femme,"* etc.). The last such book, the second half of its pages blank, has two more items in that pocket: a browned ginkgo leaf, now torn, and a folded clipping from the *Observer* for Sunday, April 10 (Nabokov's birthday by the old style), 1977, with Anthony Burgess's article "Christ the Man."

The next to last entry, on May 19, records a mildly delirious dream. In the afternoon he takes his temperature and finds that he is running a slight fever (37.5°C); disheartened, he exclaims in Russian, "*neuzheli vsio snachala?*" [oh no, not all over again!], meaning the prospect of yet another hospitalization. This came a few weeks later, and the very last entry, of June 16, is a list of toiletries he packs to take along, and also a supply of Rohypnol, a strong oneiric sedative, still illegal in the U.S., one of whose street names is "forget-me drug."

These diary records did not presume a reader, at least not in this unedited and unpolished state. The dream excerpts from Nabokov's letters to his wife, given below, obviously presupposed one (and only one, I think) reader and thus were better shaped. And the few dreams he inserted in his memoirs, placed at the end of this chapter, are composed with the same care as anything in his fiction, only they are his real dreams as far as he could recall them.

PRIOR TO THE EXPERIMENT

[1951]

1.   January 11

Dream around 7 A.M.: with V., A.,[1] other people looking from window of Rumanian queen's palace where we live, at troops (field-grey, rather old-fashioned guns, old shaggy or horribly ribby horses) passing along street, first morning of

---

1. This could be Anna Feigin (see p. 70, note 58).

revolution, sort of parade. V. contemptuous of their appearance, A. says in awe "but they are the former *Royal* guards."
V. says she doesn't care, sweeps portrait of king off console,
smashing portrait, I wander out onto balcony, drizzle, railing wet and shiny,[2] oldish queen sits there quietly looking
at passing army wet canons, wet-dark jades. Can she really
feel no sentimental thrill, no emotion whatsoever (yesterday's glory, her [dead?] husband's guardsmen)? Woke up
on question mark.

There is not a single phrase or detail in what I remember
of the dream (it was much longer anteriorly)[3] that I cannot
explain by chance impressions and thoughts I had recently;
but over it or under it there is a kind of murmur of mystery
that I cannot explain. Street was rather like street in Prague—
viewed from my mother's apartment in the early twenties.
This morning Solntzev sent me some of her letters he had
salvaged in Paris.[4]

■ *The plot and setting recur in a number of Nabokov fictions,*
especially in Pnin*'s chapter 4 (it also rains there at the beginning*
during the revolution and at the end, within and without Victor's
and Pnin's interfused dreams) and in Pale Fire.

It is strange, but agreeable with what can be often observed
in his later experiment, that Nabokov fails to mention here—

---

2. A cast-iron balcony with wet railing appears in the same notebook two weeks
afterward, in a sketch for his short story "Three Tenses," never fleshed out (but used
twenty years later in *Transparent Things*).

3. Cf. the classical French Revolution dream that Florensky adduces (p. 18)

4. Konstantin Solntzev (1894–1961), a bibliophile and philanthropist, later
professor at Syracuse University. Nabokov had not known him before 1949, when
he received a letter from Solntzev informing him that some of his papers were in
VN's possession, including some letters from VN's mother. For more on this see *V.*
V. Nabokov: Pro et Contra, vol. 2. (St. Petersburg: The Russian Christian Institute for
the Humanities, 2001), 84–87.

possibly fails to recall—that his grandmother, Baroness Maria
von Korff, was invited, after her son, Nabokov's father, was
killed in Berlin, to Rumania by the Queen and died in Bucharest
in 1925.

11.   January 16

Somewhere in the W. States, burnt-leopard type of Artemi-
sian zone (dark pattern of sage on redsoil)[5] but simultaneously in the environ of Prague Czechoslovia [*sic*], was collecting butterflies in a vividly colored dream. Family (dead
and live people) vaguely somewhere around. No butterflies
flying (as almost *always* in my collecting dreams, though I
do catch somehow some—settled on flowers etc.—probably
easier to stage on the part of the dream producer).[6] Then we
return home (in the Petersburg sense) and I notice (with my
Ithaca eyes) that E. K.[7] looks as she looked thirty-five years
ago and wears a pretty black dress. I mention the matter to
her, with difficulty, tongue turning thickly in mouth (perhaps because I always misspell tongue)[8] and feel I should
not do so.

After some kind of meal, in frantic haste to go out again on
the same hot hills with my net, search and search (probably
because my bladder is full) for my white cap, remembering
how uncomfortable I was without it in the desert sun.

NB: dreams seem to come out in more detail and to be
better recalled, since I started setting them down (like firms
sending you their publicity after you bought something).

5. A large number of moth species, all monofagous, feed on Artemisia plants.
6. A favorite Nabokov trope, his short story "Assistant Producer" (1943) being
in a sense an extended essay on the metaphor.
7. Evgenia Konstantinovna Hofeld (1884–1957), his mother's long-standing
companion.
8. Here, too: he gets it right on the third try.

7.45 A.M.

Dream: am passing by door from behind which hear slow laborious soft unsteady music. Open door. Recognize room in our St Petersburg home (but there was no piano in that room). My father—the lonely, melancholy, awkward player (but he did not play in life; if he could pick and peck a few notes, did it at even a slower rate than this); seem to know it is Mozart's second sonata that V. plays but sounds quite vague and old. Recognize him by the bald back of his head— resemblance to Karpovich[9]—and this <is> unpleasant, puts me off, in boyhood would have tiptoed up and kissed him on his bald spot. He turns sadly towards me, large limp hand on keys, other in lap. Upon noticing name "Rodolph" in partitura, which I thumb through (slightly embarrassed, not accustomed to see him, who was always so vigorously gay, in this depressed state) start speaking of the trouble I recently had of ascertaining the age of characters in "Mme Bovary."[10] By the way—I go on—how jarring it is to find in Turgenev somewhere:

"On the opposite side of the street there went a little old man of about forty-five."[11] He does not understand, looks puzzled in tired listless way. "Well, I explain brightly, because I am now almost fifty-two." Still looks puzzled, sad, benevolent and puzzled. I wake up. He was my age when he was killed.

9. Mikhail Karpovich: see p. 87, note 87.

10. Nabokov analyzed Flaubert's novel in his course on literary masterpieces, taught at Cornell from 1949 on.

11. There is a close enough passage in Turgenev's *Nest of the Gentlefolk* (1859): "Next to her was sitting a wizened, jaundiced woman of about forty-five, in a low-cut dress and a black toque, with a toothless smile on her tense, worried, and vacuous face . . ." Pavel Kirsanov, a character in his *Fathers and Sons* (1860), which Nabokov also taught at Cornell, is also "a man of about forty-five."

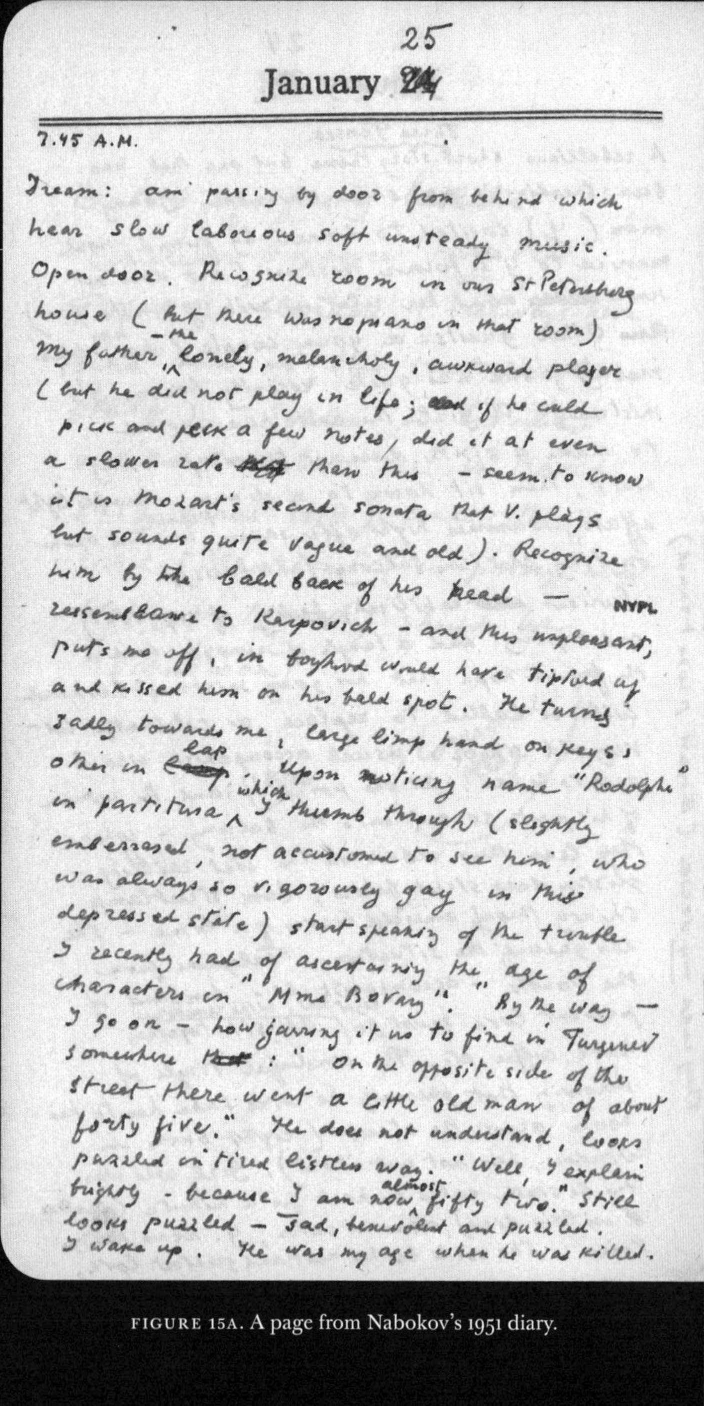

7.45 A.M.

Dream: am passing by door from behind which
hear slow laborious soft unsteady music.
Open door. Recognize room in our St Petersburg
house (but there was no piano in that room)
my father lonely, melancholy, awkward player
(but he did not play in life; and if he could
pick and peck a few notes, did it at even
a slower rate than this — seem to know
it is Mozart's second sonata that V. plays
but sounds quite vague and old). Recognize
him by the bald back of his head —
resemblance to Karpovich — and this unpleasant;
puts me off, in boyhood would have tiptoed up
and kissed him on his bald spot. He turns
sadly towards me, large limp hand on keys;
skin in lap. Upon noticing name "Rodolphe"
in partitura which I thumb through (slightly
embarrassed, not accustomed to see him, who
was always so vigorously gay in this
depressed state) start speaking of the trouble
I recently had of ascertaining the age of
characters in " Mme Bovary". " By the way —
I go on — how jarring it is to find in Turgenev
somewhere that : " on the opposite side of the
street there went a little old man of about
forty five." He does not understand, looks
puzzled in tired listless way. " Well, I explain
busyly - because I am now almost fifty two." Still
looks puzzled — Sad, benevolent and puzzled.
I wake up. He was my age when he was killed.

FIGURE 15A. A page from Nabokov's 1951 diary.

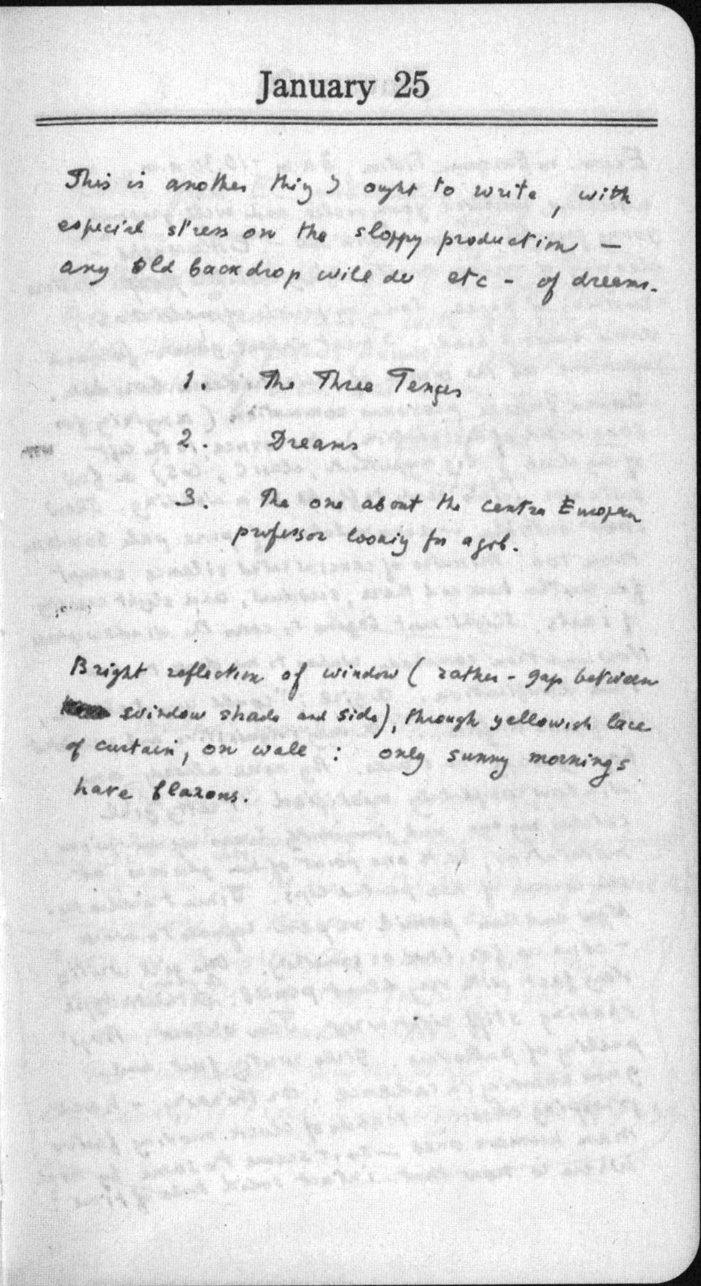

January 25

This is another thing I ought to write, with especial stress on the sloppy production — any old backdrop will do etc - of dreams.

      1.   The Three Tenses

      2.   Dreams

      3.   The one about the central European professor looking for a girl.

Bright reflection of window (rather - gap between window shade and side), through yellowish lace of curtain, on wall : only sunny mornings have flarons.

FIGURE 15B. "This is another thing I ought to write. . . ."

■ *The age coincidence is exact almost to the day: V. D. Nabokov was ninety-two days short of his fifty-second birthday when he was killed on March 28, 1922; his son, when he had this dream, was at an eighty-eight-day remove from his fifty-two. Cf. Dream 38 and also Fyodor Godunov-Cherdyntsev's dream in the last chapter of* The Gift.

IV.   March 25

Dream: am attempting a cold and joyless copulation with a fat old woman (whom I know slightly and for whom I have as much desire as for a gorilla or a garbage can). The day before somebody in my presence was telling somebody that a third party, a man I know, was—for goodness' sake—marrying a "fat old woman" whom I did not know, but whose name sounded rather like that of the one I dreamt of the night after.

March 23

Dreams: when young "forgot to put on pants," *now* "forgot to put on dentures."
Another idea:
In our dreams we are in the normal state of rudimentary man, on the eve of its being transferred into the genus *Homo*. Not *sapiens* but "awake" would be a better name for man's present condition.

[1963]

V.   May. 27 Monday. Dreamed that Kerenski was dead.[12]

---

12. Alexander Kerenski, a Russian Socialist revolutionary, prime minister of the Provisional Government from July to October 1917, died in New York in 1970.

March 25

Dream: am attempting a cold and joyless copulation with a fat old woman (whom I know slightly and for whom I have as much desire as for a gorilla or a garbage-can). The day before somebody in my presence was telling somebody that a third party, a man I know, was – for goodness' sake – ~~marrying~~ marrying a "fat old woman" whom I did not know, but whose name sounded rather like that of the one I dreamt of the night after.

AFTER THE EXPERIMENT

[1965]

VI.   April 23, *мое рождение* [my birthday]

Dream
 My name is Austin Tailor! cries woman from newsstand
where I had asked for Rumanian paper but then for NyTimes
(and finally realize she had given me Pall Mall something).

[1966]

VII.   January 7

Dream: the solution of the supreme mystery which we learn
after death is that the cosmos with all its galaxies is a blue
drop in the hollow of my palm (thus deprived of all the ter-
rors of infinity). Simple.

VIII.   April 3, 7.30 AM

Dream end: George Hessen[13] telling latest anecdote, its
"point" being street children replying to social worker: "let's
go to Seven Chops"—a disreputable dilapidated part of the
town in the dream.

[1971]

IX.   March 11

Покинуть все—работу, нѣгу,
искусство, милую скудель!

13. George Hessen (1902–1971), translator, VN's close friend.

По вечерѣющему снѣгу
такъ Пушкинъ ѣхалъ на дуэль.

Half of it in dream.

Leave everything—work, pleasure,
Art's precious brittleness?
Over the snow that flushed pink, thus
Pushkin was driving to the duel.[14]

[1973]

6 Jan 1973   X.

Dream: my father had come with Dm. and me to the
beach (there was, it turned out, a southern sea behind our
Montreux Palace). Dm. and I were worried that my father
(looking very gloomy and uncomfortable) would get badly
sunburnt.

Jan 9   XI.

Dream: Railway station in Italian city. V & I have been shop-
ping. Are about to take a local train back to our mountain
resort. I'm buttonholed on the platform by an American
tourist. V. calls me as she boards the train. I get rid of the
bore too late the train has gone. There's another soon but I
can't recall the name of the resort. It begins with A—that's
all I know. Unhelpfully helpful station master. I cannot remember the Italian for "time table" but he keeps showing
me long lists of complex freight car numbers. I wake up in
angry panic.

14. Nabokov translated that "versicle," as he called it, later, on October 15, 1975.

XII.   Jan 9

Woke up at dawn. With diurnal part of brain still in dream gear. "That's it!" I thought grimly as I sat up and saw that in the space between bed and window TWO guillotines, facing each other, had already been set ("That's the way they do it, of course—in one's bedroom"). Vertical and horizontal shadows in the barred and broken twilight, that I can never get accustomed to, kept imitating the horrible machines for at least five seconds. I had even time to wonder if V. in the adjacent bedroom was being prepared to join me. I should get thick curtains but I don't like to wait for sleep in total darkness.

XIII.   October 10

Queer dream on threshold of awakening. Was reminding A. Zak[15] of the word games we played when he was my pupil 50 years ago and invented a new specimen which I managed to carry into consciousness:

МаЙЕРУ С АЛИМентами не повезло.

■ *The Russian phrase reads "Meyer had bad luck with alimonies"; the capital letters yield the word "Jerusalem." A roughly similar English wordplay can be shown in "No more sleep-walking-related inJURIES—A LIMited time offer."*

The day before, Nabokov mailed five hundred dollars to the Israeli ambassador in Berne, "a small contribution to your country's defence against the Arabolshevist aggressors." Mark the portmanteau. The third Arab-Israeli war began October 6 that year.

15. Alexander Zak (1910–?), VN's pupil in Berlin.

[1975]

June 17

XIV.

Dream: passing across football field where Pélé <*sic*> is kicking the ball about. Shoots it towards me with strong twist. I goal lunge—and almost break my hand against bedside table.

[1976]

April 24

XV.

At 1 AM was roused from brief sleep by horrible anguish of the "this-is-it" sort. *Discreetly* screamed, hoping to wake Vé in the next room, yet fearing to succeed (because I felt quite all right).

IN LETTERS TO WIFE

■ *The following surprisingly few dream descriptions do not include very frequent "I've seen you in my dream" instances.*

"I dreamt of you last night—as if I was playing the piano and you were turning the pages for me . . ." (12 Jan. 1924)

"I dreamt that I was walking along the Palace Embankment with someone, the water in the Neva is lead-coloured, flowing thickly, and there are masts, masts without end, large boats and small ones, colourful stripes of black pipes—and I say to my companion: "The Bolsheviks have such a big fleet!" And he replies: "Yes, that's why they had to remove the bridges." After that we walked around the Winter Palace, and for some reason it was purple all over—and I thought that I must note this down for a short story. We stepped out into the Palace

Square—it was squeezed from all sides by buildings, some kind of fantastic lights were playing. And my entire dream was lit up by some threatening light—the kind you find in battle paintings." (16.6.1926)

■ *Nabokov's terse response to "Your most memorable dream" question, from a literary salon-type questionnaire (in Berlin in 1926), was: "Russia."*

"When I was little, I always used to dream of an enormous flood: so that I could take a boat ride down Morskaya, make a turn. . . . Street-lamps are sticking out of the water, further on, a hand sticks out: I approach it—and it turns out to be Peter's bronze hand!" (*2 July 1926*—NB. The last item of his cryptogram—"So long!")

"As for the question, 'What is your most memorable dream?' both Gurevich and I happened to write the same thing: Russia." (17 July 1926)

"I dreamt that my little boy was sick, and stepped out of the dream as if out of hot salted water. I love you." (17.2.1936)

"I dreamt last night that my little one was walking towards me along the pavement, with dirty cheeks, for some reason, and in a dark little coat; I ask him about myself: "Who is it?" and he replies: Volodya Nabokov, with a cunning little smile." (15.5.1937)

"This morning I was awoken by an unusually lively dream: Ilyusha (I think it was he) walks in and says that he'd been informed by phone that Khodasevich "has ended his earthly existence"—word for word." (9 June 1939, the last recorded dream in his letters to his wife)

■ *Compared to either the original* Conclusive Evidence *(1951) or to the enlarged* Speak, Memory *(1965), the Russian version of Nabokov's novelized autobiography entitled* Drugie berega *(Other Shores, 1954) differs significantly: some passages are missing, others were written specially for it and are unavailable in English. In the extensive passage concerning his early struggle with insomnia given below, the Russian text is much richer in detail; the two major insertions, in italics, are given in my translation. It is most interesting to note that whereas in later years Nabokov would not be able to fall asleep when even the dimmest light reached him in his bed (cf., for example, detailed description of his tussle with curtains in his last novel given in part 4 of this book, p. 128), in his childhood the exact opposite, total impenetrable darkness, was his dreaded nightly torment.*

All my life I have been a poor go-to-sleeper. *All my life I went to sleep with the greatest of difficulties and with disgust. A fellow train passenger who puts aside a newspaper and without any trouble is snoring the next moment is as incomprehensible to me as are people who, say, "run for an office," or enter a masonic lodge, or join any organization in order to dissolve in them energetically. I know that sleep is good for us, yet I can't get accustomed to this betrayal of one's reasoning, to that nightly and rather grotesque breaking up with one's consciousness. In later years it felt somewhat like the feeling before surgery with full anesthesia, but in my childhood the forthcoming sleep appeared as a masked executioner. . . .* No matter how great my weariness, the wrench of parting with consciousness is unspeakably repulsive to me. I loathe Somnus, that black-masked headsman binding me to the block; and if in the course of years I have got so used to my nightly ordeal as almost to swagger while the familiar axe is coming out of its great velvet-lined case, initially I had no such comfort or defense: I had nothing—save a door left slightly ajar into Mademoiselle's room. Its vertical line of meek light was something I could cling to, since in absolute darkness my head would swim, just as the soul dissolves in the blackness of sleep.

Saturday night used to be a pleasurable prospect because that was the night Mademoiselle indulged in the luxury of a weekly bath, thus granting a longer lease to my tenuous gleam. But then a subtler torture set in. The nursery bathroom in our St. Petersburg house was at the end of a Z-shaped corridor some twenty heartbeats' distance from my bed, and between dreading Mademoiselle's return from the bathroom to her lighted bedroom and envying my brother's stolid snore, I could never really put my additional time to profit by deftly getting to sleep while a chink in the dark still bespoke a speck of myself in nothingness. At length they would come, those inexorable steps, plodding along the passage and causing some little glass object, which had been secretly sharing my vigil, to tinkle in dismay on its shelf. Now she has entered her room. A brisk interchange of light values tells me that the candle on her bed table takes over the job of the lamp on her desk. My line of light is still there, but it has grown old and wan, and flickers whenever Mademoiselle makes her bed creak by moving. For I still hear her. Now it is a silvery rustle spelling "Suchard"; now the trk-trk-trk of a fruit knife cutting the pages of La Revue des Deux Mondes. I hear her panting slightly. And all the time I am in acute distress, desperately trying to coax sleep, opening my eyes every few seconds to check the faded gleam, and imagining paradise as a place where a sleepless neighbor reads an endless book by the light of an eternal candle.

The inevitable happens: the pince-nez case shuts with a snap, the review shuffles onto the marble of the bed table, and gustily Mademoiselle's pursed lips blow; the first attempt fails, a groggy flame squirms and ducks; then comes a second lunge, and light collapses. In that pitchy blackness I lose my bearings, my bed seems to be slowly drifting, panic makes me sit up and stare. *Lord, don't they know that I can't sleep without a point of light—that raving madness and death are nothing else but this perfectly black blackness! But gradually* my dark-adapted eyes sift out, among entoptic floaters, certain more precious blurrings that roam in aimless amnesia until, half-remembering, they settle down as the dim folds of window curtains behind which streetlights are remotely alive. ("Mademoiselle O.")[16]

16. *Stories*, 488.

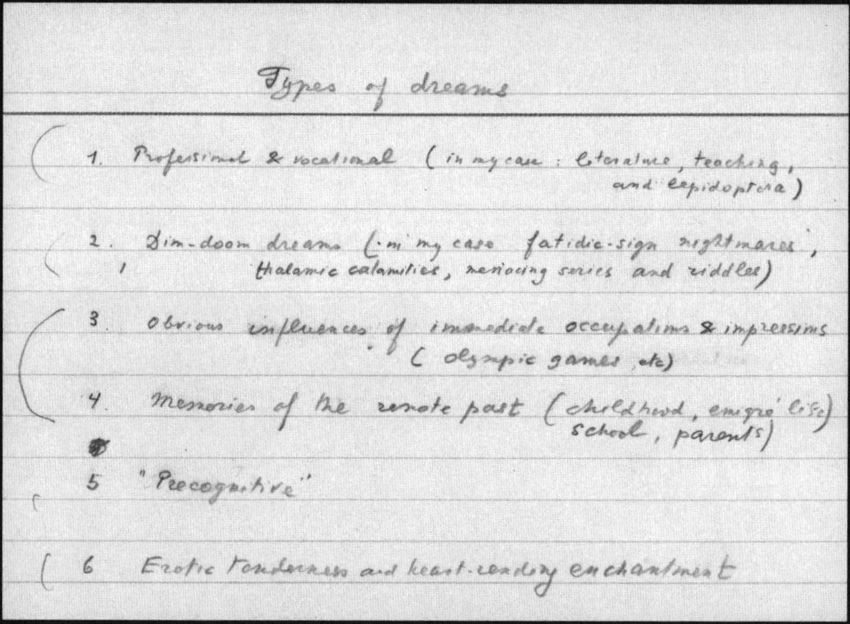

Types of dreams

1. Professional & vocational (in my case : literature, teaching, and lepidoptera)

2. Dim-doom dreams (in my case fatidic-sign nightmares, thalamic calamities, menacing series and riddles)

3. Obvious influences of immediate occupations & impressions (olympic games, etc)

4. Memories of the remote past (childhood, emigré life, school, parents)

5. "Precognitive"

6. Erotic tenderness and heart-rending enchantment

FIGURE 17. This card, listing "Types of Dreams," appears among the dream records on a separate, undated card following the December 6, 1964, dream (most likely misplaced later).

PART 4

THE ART OF DREAMING

THE ADJECTIVE "DREAMY" (*mechtatel'nyi*, daydreaming, in Russian) is one of the most often used nuancers in Nabokov's palette. In chapter 4 of the second part of *Ada* the nonagenarian Van Veen summarizes his dream life in what appears to be the closest we have got to a treatise of Nabokov's dream theory and classification, influenced to a considerable degree by his 1964 experiment. It is worth giving here in its entirety, since Van's examples match well the categories described here.

What are dreams? A random sequence of scenes, trivial or tragic, viatic or static, fantastic or familiar, featuring more or less plausible events patched up with grotesque details, and recasting dead people in new settings.

In reviewing the more or less memorable dreams I have had during the last nine decades I can classify them by subject matter into several categories among which two surpass the others in generic distinctiveness. There are the professional dreams and there are the erotic ones. In my twenties the first kind occurred about as frequently as the second, and both had their introductory counterparts, insomnias conditioned either by the overflow of ten hours of vocational work or by the memory of Ardis that a thorn in my day had maddeningly revived. After work I battled against the might of the mind-set: the stream of composition, the force of the phrase demanding to be formed could not be stopped for hours of darkness and discomfort, and when some result had been achieved, the current still hummed on and on behind the wall, even if I locked up my brain by an act of self-hypnosis (plain will, or pill, could no longer help) within some other image or meditation—but not Ardis, not Ada, for that would mean drowning in a cataract of worse wakefulness, with rage and regret, desire and despair sweeping me into an abyss where sheer physical extenuation stunned me at last with sleep.

In the professional dreams that especially obsessed me when I worked on my earliest fiction, and pleaded abjectly with a very frail muse ('kneeling and wringing my hands' like the dusty-trousered Marmlad before his Marmlady in Dickens), I might see for example that I was correcting galley proofs but that somehow (the great 'somehow' of dreams!) the book had already come out, had come out literally, being proffered to me by a human hand from the wastepaper basket in its perfect, and dreadfully imperfect, stage—with a typo on every page, such as the snide 'bitterly' instead of 'butterfly' and the meaningless 'nuclear' instead of 'unclear.' Or I would be hurrying to a reading I had to give—would feel exasperated by the sight of the traffic and people blocking my way, and then realize with sudden relief that all I had to do was to strike out the phrase 'crowded street' in my manuscript. What I might designate as 'skyscape' (not 'skyscrape,' as two-thirds of the class will probably take it down) dreams belongs to a subdivision of my vocational visions, or perhaps may represent a preface to them, for it was in my early pubescence that hardly a night would pass without some old or recent waketime impression's establishing a soft deep link with my still-muted genius (for we are 'van,' rhyming with and indeed signifying 'one' in Marina's double-you-less deep-voweled Russian pronunciation). The presence, or promise, of art in that kind of dream would come in the image of an overcast sky with a manifold lining of cloud, a motionless but hopeful white, a hopeless but gliding gray, showing artistic signs of clearing, and presently the glow of a pale sun grew through the leaner layer only to be recowled by the scud, for I was not yet ready.

Allied to the professional and vocational dreams are 'dim-doom' visions: fatidic-sign nightmares, thalamic calamities, menacing riddles. Not infrequently the menace is well concealed, and the innocent incident will turn out to possess, if jotted down and looked up later, the kind of precognitive flavor that Dunne has explained by the action of 'reverse memory'; but for the moment I am not going to enlarge upon the uncanny element particular to dreams—beyond observing that some law of logic should fix the number of coincidences, in a given domain, after which they cease to be coincidences, and form, instead, the living organism of a new truth ('Tell me,' says Osberg's little gitana to the Moors, El Motela and Ramera, 'what is the precise minimum of hairs on a body that allows one to call it "hairy"'?).

Between the dim-doom and the poignantly sensual, I would place 'melts' of erotic tenderness and heart-rending enchantment, chance frôlements of anonymous girls at vague parties, half-smiles of appeal or submission—forerunners or echoes of the agonizing dreams of regret when series of receding Adas faded away in silent reproach; and tears, even hotter than those I would shed in waking life, shook and scalded poor Van, and were remembered at odd moments for days and weeks.

Van's sexual dreams are embarrassing to describe in a family chronicle that the very young may perhaps read after a very old man's death. Two samples, more or less euphemistically worded, should suffice. In an intricate arrangement of thematic recollections and automatic phantasmata, Aqua impersonating Marina or Marina made-up to look like Aqua, arrives to inform Van, joyfully, that Ada has just been delivered of a girl-child whom he is about to know carnally on a hard garden bench while under a nearby pine, his father, or his dress-coated mother, is trying to make a transatlantic call for an ambulance to be sent from Vence at once. Another dream, recurring in its basic, unmentionable form, since 1888 and well into this century, contained an essentially triple and, in a way, tribadic, idea. Bad Ada and lewd Lucette had found a ripe, very ripe ear of Indian corn. Ada held it at both ends as if it were a mouth organ and now it was an organ, and she moved her parted lips along it, varnishing its shaft, and while she was making it trill and moan, Lucette's mouth engulfed its extremity. The two sisters' avid lovely young faces were now close together, doleful and wistful in their slow, almost languid play, their tongues meeting in flicks of fire and curling back again, their tumbled hair, red-bronze and black-bronze, delightfully commingling and their sleek hindquarters lifted high as they slaked their thirst in the pool of his blood.

I have some notes here on the general character of dreams. One puzzling feature is the multitude of perfect strangers with clear features, but never seen again, accompanying, meeting, welcoming me, pestering me with long tedious tales about other strangers—all this in localities familiar to me and in the midst of people, deceased or living, whom I knew well; or the curious tricks of an agent of Chronos—a very exact clock-time awareness, with all the pangs (possibly full-bladder pangs in disguise) of not getting somewhere in time, and with that clock hand before me, numerically meaningful, mechanically plausible, but combined—and that is the curious part—with an extremely hazy, hardly existing passing-of-time feeling (this theme I will also reserve for a later chapter). All dreams are affected by the experiences and impressions of the present as well as by memories of childhood; all reflect, in images or sensations, a draft, a light, a rich meal or a grave internal disorder. Perhaps the most typical trait of practically all dreams, unimportant or portentous—and this despite the presence, in stretches or patches, of fairly logical (within special limits) cogitation and awareness (often absurd) of dream-past events—should be understood by my students as a dismal weakening of the intellectual faculties of the dreamer, who is not really shocked to run into a long-dead friend. At his best the dreamer wears semi-opaque blinkers; at his worst he's an imbecile. The class (1891, 1892, 1893, 1894, et cetera) will carefully note (rustle of bluebooks) that, owing to their very nature, to that mental mediocrity and bumble, dreams cannot yield any semblance of morality or symbol or allegory or Greek myth, unless, naturally, the dreamer is a Greek or a mythicist. Metamorphoses in dreams are as common as metaphors in poetry. A writer who likens, say, the fact of imagination's weakening less rapidly than memory, to the lead of a pencil getting used up more slowly than its erasing end, is comparing two real, concrete, existing things. Do you want me to repeat that? (cries of 'yes! yes!') Well, the pencil I'm holding is still conveniently long though it has served me a lot, but its rubber cap is practically erased by the very action it has been performing too many times. My imagination is still strong and serviceable but my memory is getting shorter and shorter. I compare that real experience to the condition of this real commonplace object. Neither is a symbol of the other. Similarly, when a teashop humorist says that a little conical titbit with a comical cherry on top resembles this or that (titters in the audience) he is turning a pink cake into a pink breast (tempestuous laughter) in a fraise-like frill or frilled phrase (silence). Both objects are real, they are not interchangeable, not tokens of something else, say, of Walter Raleigh's decapitated trunk still topped by the image of his wetnurse (one lone chuckle). Now the mistake—the lewd, ludicrous and vulgar mistake of the Signy-Mondieu analysts consists in their regarding a real object, a pompon, say, or a pumpkin (actually seen in a dream by the patient) as a significant abstraction of the real object, as a bumpkin's bonbon or one-half of the bust if you see what I mean (scattered giggles). There can be no emblem or parable in a village idiot's hallucinations or in last night's dream of any of us in this hall. In those random visions nothing—underscore 'nothing' (grating sound of horizontal strokes)—can be construed as allowing itself to be deciphered by a witch doctor who can then cure a madman or give comfort to a killer by laying the blame on a too fond, too fiendish or too indifferent parent— secret festerings that the foster quack feigns to heal by expensive confession fests (laughter and applause).[1]

In an introductory note to his experiment, Nabokov subdivides his usual dreams thematically into six rough types (see the list on page 34). Yet even the dreams he sees during the

1. *Ada*, 361–64.

experiment do not fit these six categories neatly. Is jumping into a ditch during shooting in an unknown town (#36) a fatidic dream? Can seeing Edmund Wilson making, in a "Lausanne-like railway station," a critical comment of Nabokov's would-be peculiarly "Russian" usage of the word "upstairs" (#46), half-a-year prior to their famous public falling-out over Wilson's feeble but presumptive command of Russian, be a precognitive dream? Or simply associative with Wilson's *To the Finland Station*, published in 1940, the year when Nabokov first met him and politely dismissed Wilson's left-wing political naïveté on display in that book? Is every "erotic" dream of his so tender and enchanting (e.g., #IV)? Can he know a "precognitive" dream when he sees one (the point of Dunne's experiment, of course)?

I therefore had to add a few new type-models in this section and some variations into Nabokov's. For example, it seems inadequate to label dreams visited by his father (#38, or 25 Jan. 1951, #III) as mere "memories of the remote past": his father appears in a faintly unfamiliar guise, unsmiling, remote, even morose, as though his present mysterious after-death condition made the change of attitude inevitable, painful as it may be for his son. And when Nabokov's characters dream of their fathers, they often experience a similar sensation of awe, enigma, and dread, nowhere staged as masterfully and vividly as in the tremendous passage from *The Gift*, given here in full.

A subspecies within each type is named in brackets. It is often difficult to place a passage under a thematic rubric: it may straddle more than one or even two, or, conversely, it may require for itself a subtler subsection. In fiction, Nabokov staged his characters' dreams, composing them from the pieces of his own dreaming experience (memory) and those custom-made for the occasion (imagination). Within a given category, dreams culled from fiction are ordered by ascending chronology.

The original Russian text important to the thematic section, but left out in translation by oversight or on purpose, is inserted in angle brackets (in my rendition); important additions made in an English version are italicized.

The excerpts below do not include examples from Nabokov's plays. Most of them are conceived and set as Calderonic dreams. In the early masterpiece *The Tragedy of Mr. Morn* (1924), the curtain rises on a character slumbering in an armchair, whose first words upon waking up are "Dream, fever, dream . . ."; indeed, the entire drama turns out to be a dream of a "foreign author" who visits the scene of his fantasy. The late *The Event* (1938) leaves a like suspicion that either the play is a dream or else life is, since the two protagonists are given sometimes to see an "exit" sign dimly lit outside of their nightmare. And in his last play, *The Waltz Invention*, the chief dramatic persona is a sleeping persona; in fact, "Dream" (renamed "Trance" in translation) is the most important actor and stage director.

PROFESSIONAL

Dreams related to the writer's craft,
particularly verbal manipulation

He resembled somewhat Bouteillan as the latter had been ten years ago and as he had appeared in a dream, which Van now retrostructed as far as it would go: in it Demon's former valet explained to Van that the 'dor' in the name of an adored river equaled the corruption of hydro in 'dorophone.' Van often had word dreams. (*Ada,* 309)

Somebody said, wheeling a table nearby: "It's one of the Vane sisters," and he awoke murmuring with professional appreciation the oneiric word-play combining his name and surname, and plucked out the wax plugs. (*Ada,* 521)

DOOM

Dreams displaying supposed signs of
impending disaster, especially death

He came to in the middle of the room, awakened by a sense of unbearable horror. The horror had knocked him off the bed. He had dreamt that the wall next to which stood his bed had begun slowly collapsing onto him—so he had recoiled with a spasmodic exhalation. ("Wingstroke," *Stories*, 32)

Recently, in her sleep, she had had a vision of a dead youth with whom, before she was married, she had strolled in the twilight, when the blackberry blooms seem so ghostly white. Next morning, still as if half-asleep, she had penciled a letter to him—a letter to her dream. In this letter she had lied to poor Jack. She had, in fact, nearly forgotten about him; she loved her excruciating husband with a fearful but faithful love; yet she wanted to send a little warmth to this dear spectral visitor, to reassure him with some words from earth. The letter vanished mysteriously from her writing pad, and the same night she dreamt of a long table, from under which Jack suddenly emerged, nodding to her gratefully. . . . Now, for some reason, she felt uneasy when recalling that dream . . . As if she had cheated on her husband with a ghost . . . ("Revenge," *Stories*, 70)

And once he dreamt he saw Turati sitting with his back to him. Turati was deep in thought, leaning on one arm, but from behind his broad back it was impossible to see what it was he was bending over and pondering. Luzhin did not want to see what it was, afraid to see, but nonetheless he cautiously began to look over the black shoulder. And then he saw that a bowl of soup stood before Turati and that he was not leaning on his arm but was merely tucking a napkin into his collar. And on the November day which this dream preceded Luzhin was married. (*The Defense*, 177)

Sleep imperceptibly took advantage of this happiness and relief but now, in sleep, there was no rest at all, for sleep consisted of sixty-four squares, a gigantic board in the middle of which, trembling and stark-naked, Luzhin stood, the size of a pawn, and peered at the dim positions of huge pieces, <humpbacked>, megacephalous, with crowns or manes. (*The Defense*, 236)

Sometimes in his dreams he swore to the doctor with the agate eyes that he was not playing chess—he had merely set out the pieces once on a pocket board and glanced at two or three games printed in the newspapers—simply for lack of something to do. (*The Defense*, 241–42)

False Predictors

She believed in dreams: to dream you had lost a tooth portended the death of someone you knew; and if there came blood with the tooth, then it would be the death of a relative. A field of daisies foretold meeting again one's first lover. Pearls stood for tears. It was very bad to see oneself all in white sitting at the head of the table. Mud meant money; a cat—treason; the sea-trouble for the soul. She was fond of recounting her dreams, circumstantially and at length. (*Despair*, 32)

Recurrent

For several years I was haunted by a very singular and very nasty dream: I dreamed I was standing in the middle of a long passage with a door at the bottom, and passionately wanting, but not daring to go and open it, and then deciding at last to go, which I accordingly did; but at once awoke with a groan, for what I saw there was unimaginably terrible; to wit, a perfectly empty, newly whitewashed room. That was all, but it was so terrible that I never could hold out; then one night a chair and its slender shadow appeared in the middle of the bare room—not as a first item of furniture but as though somebody had brought it to climb upon it and fix a bit of drapery, and since I knew whom I would find there next time stretching up with a hammer and a mouthful of nails, I spat them out and never opened that door again. (*Despair*, 56–57)

. . . instead of writing I went out of doors again, roaming till late, and when I returned, I was so utterly fagged out, that sleep overcame me at once, despite the confused discomfort of my mind. I dreamt that after a tedious search (offstage— not shown in my dream) I at last found Lydia, who was hiding from me and who now coolly declared that all was well, she had got the inheritance all right and was going to marry another man, "because, you see," she said, "you are dead." I woke up in a terrific rage, my heart pounding madly: fooled! helpless!—for how could a dead man sue the living—yes, helpless—and she knew it! Then I came to my wits again and laughed—what humbugs dreams are liable to be. (*Despair*, 209–210)

Message Unrecognized

Atavistic peace came with dawn, and when I slipped into sleep the sun through the tawny window shades penetrated a dream that somehow was full of Cynthia.

This was disappointing. Secure in the fortress of daylight, I said to myself that I had expected more. She, a painter of glass-bright minutiae—and now so vague! I lay in bed, thinking my dream over and listening to the sparrows outside: Who knows, if recorded and then run backward, those bird sounds might not become human speech, voiced words, just as the latter become a twitter when reversed? I set myself to reread my dream—backward, diagonally, up, down—trying hard to unravel something Cynthia-like in it, something strange and suggestive that must be there.

I could isolate, consciously, little. Everything seemed blurred, yellow-clouded, yielding nothing tangible. Her inept acrostics, maudlin evasions, theopathies—every recollection formed ripples of mysterious meaning. Everything seemed yellowly blurred, illusive, lost. ("The Vane Sisters," *Stories*, 631)

When I was a boy of seven or eight, I used to dream a vaguely recurrent dream set in a certain environment, which I have never been able to recognize and identify in any rational manner, though I have seen many strange lands. I am inclined to make it serve now, in order to patch up a gaping hole, a raw wound in my story. There was nothing spectacular about that environment, nothing monstrous or even odd: just a bit of noncommittal stability represented by a bit of level ground and filmed over with a bit of neutral nebulosity; in other words, the indifferent back of a view rather than its face. The nuisance of that dream was that for some reason I could not walk around the view to meet it on equal terms. There lurked in the mist a mass of something—mineral matter or the like—oppressively and quite meaninglessly shaped, and, in the course of my dream, I kept filling some kind of receptacle (translated as "pail") with smaller shapes (translated as "pebbles"), and my nose was bleeding but I was too impatient and excited to do anything about it. And every time I had that dream, suddenly somebody would start screaming behind me, and I awoke screaming too, thus prolonging the initial anonymous shriek, with its initial note of rising exultation, but with no meaning attached to it any more—if there had been a meaning. Speaking of Lance, I would like to submit that something on the lines of my dream— But the funny thing is that as I reread what I have set down, its background, the factual memory vanishes—has vanished altogether by now—and I have no means of proving to myself that there is any personal experience behind its description. What I wanted to say was that perhaps Lance and his companions, when they reached their planet, felt something akin to my dream—which is no longer mine. ("Lance," *Stories*, 640–41)

And that night I dreamt a singularly unpleasant dream. I dreamt I was sitting in a large dim room which my dream had hastily furnished with odds and ends collected in different houses I vaguely knew, but with gaps or strange substitutions, as for instance that shelf which was at the same time a dusty road. I had a hazy feeling that the room was in a farmhouse or a country inn—a general impression of wooden walls and planking. We were expecting Sebastian—he was due to come back from some long journey. I was sitting on a crate or something, and my mother was also in the room, and there were two more persons drinking tea at the table round which we were seated—a man from my office and his wife, both of whom Sebastian had never known, and who had been placed there by the dream manager—just because anybody would do to fill the stage.

Our wait was uneasy, laden with obscure forebodings, and I felt that they knew more than I, but I dreaded to inquire why my mother worried so much about a muddy bicycle which refused to be crammed into the wardrobe: its doors kept opening. There was the picture of a steamer on the wall, and the waves on the picture moved like a procession of caterpillars, and the steamer rocked and this annoyed me—until I remembered that the hanging of such a picture was an old and commonplace custom, when awaiting a traveller's return.

He might arrive at any moment, and the wooden floor near the door had been sprinkled with sand, so that he might not slip. My mother wandered away with the muddy spurs and stirrups she could not hide, and the vague couple was quietly abolished, for I was alone in the room, when a door opened in a gallery upstairs, and Sebastian appeared, slowly descending a rickety flight of stairs which came straight down into the room. His hair was tousled and he was coatless: he had, I understood, just been taking a nap after his journey. As he came down, pausing a little on every step, with always the same foot ready to continue and with his arm resting on the wooden handrail, my mother came back again and helped him to get up when he stumbled and slithered down on his back. He laughed as he came up to me, but I felt that he was ashamed of something. His face was pale and unshaven, but it looked fairly cheerful. My mother, with a silver cup in her hand, sat down on what proved to be a stretcher, for she was presently carried away by two men who slept on Saturdays in the house, as Sebastian told me with a smile. Suddenly I noticed that he wore a black glove on his left hand, and that the fingers of that hand did not move, and that he never used it—I was afraid horribly, squeamishly, to the point of nausea, that he might inadvertently touch me with it, for I understood now that it was a sham thing attached to the wrist—that he had been operated upon, or had had some dreadful accident. I understood too why his appearance and the whole atmosphere of his arrival seemed so uncanny, but though he perhaps noticed my shudder, he went on with his tea. My mother came back for a moment to fetch the thimble she had forgotten and quickly went away, for the men were in a hurry. Sebastian asked me whether the manicurist had already come, as he was anxious to get ready for the banquet. I tried to dismiss the subject, because the idea of his maimed hand was insufferable, but presently I saw the whole room in terms of jagged fingernails, and a girl I had known (but she had strangely faded now) arrived with her manicure case and sat down on a stool in front of Sebastian. He asked me not to look, but I could not help looking. I saw him undoing his black glove and slowly pulling it off; and as it came off, it spilled its only contents—a number of tiny hands, like the front paws of a mouse, mauve-pink and soft—lots of them—and they dropped to the floor, and the girl in black went on her knees. I bent down to see what she was doing under the table and I saw that she was picking up the little hands and putting them into a dish—I looked up and Sebastian had vanished, and when I bent down again, the girl had vanished too. I felt I could not stay in that room for a moment longer. But as I turned and groped for the latch I heard Sebastian's voice behind me; it seemed to come from the darkest and re-motest corner of what was now an enormous barn with grain trickling out of a punctured bag at my feet. I could not see him and was so eager to escape that the throbbing of my im-patience seemed to drown the words he said. I knew he was calling me and saying something very important—and prom-ising to tell me something more important still, if only I came to the corner where he sat or lay, trapped by the heavy sacks that had fallen across his legs. I moved, and then his voice came in one last loud insistent appeal, and a phrase which made no sense when I brought it out of my dream, then, in the dream itself, rang out laden with such absolute moment, with such an unfailing intent to solve for me a monstrous riddle, that I would have run to Sebastian after all, had I not been half out of my dream already. (*The Real Life of Sebastian Knight*, 187–90)

It bristled with farcical anachronisms; it was suffused with a sense of gross maturity (as in *Hamlet* the churchyard scene); its somewhat meagre setting was patched up with odds and ends from other (later) plays; but still the recurrent dream we all know (finding ourselves in the old classroom, with our homework not done because of our having unwittingly missed ten thousand days of school) was in Krug's case a fair rendering of the atmosphere of the original version. Naturally, the script of daytime memory is far more subtle in regard to factual details, since a good deal of cutting and trimming and conventional recombination has to be done by the dream producers (of whom there are usually several, mostly illiterate and middle-class and pressed by time); but a show is always a show, and the embarrassing return to one's former existence (with the off-stage passing of years translated in terms of forgetfulness, truancy, inefficiency) is somehow better enacted by a popular dream than by the scholarly precision of memory. < . . . > But among the producers or stagehands responsible for the setting there has been one . . . it is hard to express it . . . a nameless, mysterious genius who took advantage of the dream to convey his own peculiar code message which has nothing to do with school days or indeed with any aspect of Krug's physical existence, but which links him up somehow with an unfathomable mode of being, perhaps terrible, perhaps blissful, perhaps neither, a kind of transcendental madness which lurks behind the corner of consciousness and which cannot be defined more accurately than this, no matter how Krug strains his brain. (*Bend Sinister,* 55–56)

In the middle of the night something in a dream shook him out of his sleep into what was really a prison cell with bars of light (and a separate pale gleam like the footprint of some phosphorescent islander) breaking the darkness. At first, as sometimes happens, his surroundings did not match any form of reality. Although of humble origin (a vigilant arc light outside, a livid corner of the prison yard, an oblique ray coming through some chink or bullet hole in the bolted and padlocked shutters) the luminous pattern he saw assumed a strange, perhaps fatal significance, the key to which was half-hidden by a flap of dark consciousness on the glimmering floor of a half-remembered nightmare. It would seem that some promise had been broken, some design thwarted, some opportunity missed—or so grossly exploited as to leave an afterglow of sin and shame. The pattern of light was somehow the result of a kind of stealthy, abstractly vindictive, groping, tampering movement that had been going on in a dream, or behind a dream, in a tangle of immemorial and by now formless and aimless machinations. Imagine a sign that warns you of an explosion in such cryptic or childish language that you wonder whether everything—the sign, the frozen explosion under the window sill and your quivering soul—has not been reproduced artificially, there and then, by special arrangement with the mind behind the mirror.

It was at that moment, just after Krug had fallen through the bottom of a confused dream and sat up on the straw with a gasp—and just before his reality, his remembered hideous misfortune could pounce upon him—it was then that I felt a pang of pity for Adam and slid towards him along an inclined beam of pale light—causing instantaneous madness, but at least saving him from the senseless agony of his logical fate. (*Bend Sinister,* 209–10)

> For as we know from dreams it is so hard
> To speak to our dear dead! They disregard
> Our apprehension, queasiness and shame—
> The awful sense that they're not quite the same.
> And our school chum killed in a distant war
> Is not surprised to see us at his door.
> And in a blend of jauntiness and gloom
> Points at the puddles in his basement room.
>   ("Pale Fire," ll. 589–96, *Pale Fire*)

[Hugh Person dozes off as the fire is creeping up to his hotel floor.]
Here comes the air hostess bringing bright drinks, and she is
Armande who has just accepted his offer of marriage though
he warned her that she overestimated a lot of things, the plea-
sures of parties in New York, the importance of his job, a
future inheritance, his uncle's stationery business, the mountains of Vermont—and now the airplane explodes with a roar
and a retching cough. < . . . > Coughing, our Person sat up in
asphyxiating darkness and groped for the light. (*Transparent
Things*, 103)

At its worst it went like this: An hour or so after falling
asleep (generally well after midnight and with the humble assistance of a little Old Mead or Chartreuse) I would
wake up (or rather "wake in") momentarily mad. The hideous pang in my brain was triggered by some hint of faint
light in the line of my sight, for no matter how carefully I
might have topped the well-meaning efforts of a servant by
my own struggles with blinds and purblinds, there always
remained some damned slit, some atom or dimmet of artificial streetlight or natural moonlight that signaled inex-
pressible peril when I raised my head with a gasp above the
level of a choking dream. Along the dim slit brighter points
traveled with dreadful meaningful intervals between them.
Those dots corresponded, perhaps, to my rapid heartbeats or
were connected optically with the blinking of wet eyelashes
but the rationale of it is inessential; its dreadful part was
my realizing in helpless panic that the event had been stu-
pidly unforeseen, yet had been bound to happen and was the
representation of a fatidic problem which had to be solved
lest I perish and indeed might have been solved now if I
had given it some forethought or had been less sleepy and
weak-witted at this all-important moment. The problem itself was of a calculatory order: certain relations between the

twinkling points had to be measured or, in my case, guessed, since my torpor prevented me from counting them properly, let alone recalling what the safe number should be. Error meant instant retribution—beheading by a giant or worse; the right guess, per contra, would allow me to escape into an enchanting region situated just beyond the gap I had to wriggle through in the thorny riddle, a region resembling in its idyllic abstraction those little landscapes engraved as suggestive vignettes—a brook, a bosquet—next to capital letters of weird, ferocious shape such as a Gothic B beginning a chapter in old books for easily frightened children. But how could I know in my torpor and panic that this was the simple solution, that the brook and the boughs and the beauty of the Beyond all began with the initial of Being? < . . . > There were nights, of course, when my reason returned at once and I rearranged the curtains and presently slept. (*Look at the Harlequins!* 15)

■ *(An effect opposite to one in his childhood, when VN dreaded to be left at night in complete darkness, hoping for a chink of light from under the door to be let stay—cf. pp. 108–9)*

In a recurrent dream of my childhood I used to see a smudge on the wallpaper or on a whitewashed door, a nasty smudge that started to come alive, turning into a crustacean-like monster. As its appendages began to move, a thrill of foolish horror shook me awake; but the same night or the next I would be again facing idly some wall or screen on which a spot of dirt would attract the naive sleeper's attention by starting to grow and make groping and clasping gestures—and again I managed to wake up before its bloated bulk got unstuck from the wall. But one night when some trick of position, some dimple of pillow, some fold of bedclothes made me feel brighter and braver than usual, I let the smudge start its evolution and, drawing on an imagined mitten, I simply rubbed out the beast. Three or four times it appeared again in my dreams but now I welcomed its growing shape and gleefully erased it. Finally it gave up—as some day life will give up—bothering me. (*The Original of Laura*, 249–53)

DAYTIME IMPRESSIONS

Humdrum images or events of the day that
acquire significance in the subsequent dream,
disfigured or fantastically rearranged.

The Staircase was the main idol of her [Margot's] existence—not as a symbol of glorious ascension, but as a thing to be kept nicely polished, so that her worst nightmare (after too generous a helping of potatoes and sauerkraut) was a flight of white steps with the black trace of a boot first right, then left, then right again and so on—up to the top landing. (*Laughter in the Dark*, 24–25)

The original Russian version:

<In her night dreams, she [Magda] often saw a fabulously splendid, white-as-sugar staircase and a tiny silhouette of a man who had already reached the top but left a large black imprint of his sole on every step, left-right-left-right. . . . It was a painful dream.> (*Camera Obscura*, 16)

■ *In that book all three major characters have their dreams reported.*

Van managed to sleep soundly, the only reaction on the part of his dormant mind being the dream image of an aquatic peacock, slowly sinking before somersaulting like a diving grebe, near the shore of the lake bearing his name in the ancient kingdom of Arrowroot. Upon reviewing that bright dream he traced its source to his recent visit to Armenia where he had gone fowling with Armborough and that gentleman's extremely compliant and accomplished niece. He wanted to make a note of it—and was amused to find that all three pencils had not only left his bed table but had neatly aligned themselves head to tail along the bottom of the outer door of the adjacent room, having covered quite a stretch of blue carpeting in the course of their stopped escape. (*Ada*, 474–75)

MEMORIES OF THE REMOTE PAST

Then [Klara] fell asleep and had a nonsensical dream: she seemed to be sitting in a tramcar next to an old woman extraordinarily like her Lodz aunt, who was talking rapidly in German; then it gradually turned out that it was not her aunt at all but the cheerful marketwoman from whom Klara bought oranges on her way to work. (*Mary*, 37)

["Although an ass might argue that 'orange' is the oneiric anagram of organe, I would not advise members of the Viennese delegation to lose precious time analyzing Klara's dream at the end of Chapter Four in the present book." (VN's preface, *Mary*, xiii)]

He returned to his squalid hotel and, slowly stretching his intertwined hands behind his head, collapsed onto the bed in a state of blissful solar inebriation. He dreamt he was an officer again, walking along a Crimean slope overgrown with milkweed and oak shrubs, mowing off the downy heads of thistles as he went. He awoke because he had started laughing in his sleep; he awoke, and the window had already turned a twilight blue. ("The Seaport," *Stories*, 64)

(see also Insomnia, Clairvoyance, and Life Is a Dream)

His heart was thumping rapidly because he sensed that Maureen had entered his room. Just now, in his momentary dream, he had been talking to her, helping her climb the waxen path between black cliffs with their occasional glossy, oil-paint fissures. Now and then a dulcet breeze made the narrow white headdress quiver gently, like a sheet of thin paper, on her dark hair. ("La Veneziana," *Stories*, 108)

■ *This is an example of an almost perfect "Dunne's Dream": what he saw in that instantaneous dream ("he had just fallen asleep and, as sometimes happens, the very act of falling asleep was what woke him") is soon to come true in reality retrospectively, as it were—a fantastic reality, to be sure, but then that is what fiction is all about.*

To begin with, I slept badly for three nights in a row and did not sleep at all during the fourth. In recent years I had lost the habit of solitude, and now those solitary nights caused me acute unrelieved anguish. The first night I saw my girl in dream: sunlight flooded her room, and she sat on the bed wearing only a lacy nightgown, and laughed, and laughed, could not stop laughing. And I recalled my dream quite by accident, as I was passing a lingerie store, and upon remembering it realized that all that had been so gay in my dream— her lace, her thrown-back head, her laughter—was now, in my waking state, frightening. Yet I could not explain to myself why that lacy laughing dream was now so unpleasant, so hideous. ("Terror," *Stories*, 176)

Gradually Graf dozed off in his chair and in his dream he saw Ivan Ivanovich Engel singing couplets in a garden of sorts and fanning his bright-yellow, curly-feathered wings, and when Graf woke up the lovely June sun was lighting little rainbows in the landlady's liqueur glasses, and everything was somehow soft and luminous and enigmatic—as if there was something he had not understood, not thought through to the end, and now it was already too late, another life had begun, the past had withered away, and death had quite, quite removed the meaningless memory, summoned by chance from the distant and humble home where it had been living out its obscure existence. ("A Busy Man," *Stories*, 295–96)

The chambermaid did not have to wake Luzhin—he awoke by himself and immediately made strenuous efforts to recall the delightful dream he had dreamed, knowing from experience that if you didn't begin immediately to recall it, later would be too late. He had dreamed he was sitting strangely—in the middle of the room—and suddenly, with the absurd and blissful suddenness usual in dreams, his fiancée entered holding out a package tied with red ribbon. She was dressed also in the style of dreams—in a white dress and soundless white shoes. He wanted to embrace her, but suddenly felt sick, his head whirled, and she in the meantime related that the newspapers were writing extraordinary things about him but that her mother still did not want them to marry. Probably there was much more of this and that, but his memory failed to overtake what was receding—and trying at least not to disperse what he had managed to wrest from his dream, Luzhin stirred cautiously, smoothed down his hair and rang for dinner to be brought. After dinner he had to play, and that day the universe of chess concepts revealed an awesome power. He played four hours without pause and won, but when he was already sitting in the taxi he forgot on the way where it was he was going, what postcard address he had given the driver to read and waited with interest to see where the car would stop.

The house, however, he recognized, and again there were guests, guests—but here Luzhin realized that he had simply returned to his recent dream, for his fiancée asked him in a whisper: "Well, how are you, has the sickness gone?"—and how could she have known about this in real life? "We're living in a fine dream," he said to her softly. "Now I understand everything." He looked about him and saw the table and the faces of people sitting there, their reflection in the samovar—in a special samovarian perspective—and added with tremendous relief: "So this too is a dream? These people are a dream? Well, well . . ." "Quiet, quiet, what are you babbling about?" she whispered anxiously, and Luzhin thought she was right, one should not scare off a dream, let them sit there, these people, for the time being. But the most remarkable thing about this dream was that all around, evidently, was Russia, which the sleeper himself had left ages ago. The inhabitants of the dream, gay people drinking tea, were conversing in Russian and the sugar bowl was identical with the one from which he had spooned powdered sugar on the veranda on a scarlet summer evening many years ago. Luzhin noted this return to Russia with interest, with pleasure. It diverted him especially as the witty repetition of a particular combination, which occurs, for example, when a strictly problem idea, long since discovered in theory, is repeated in a striking guise on the board in live play.

The whole time, however, now feebly, now sharply, shadows of his real chess life would show through this dream and finally it broke through and it was simply night in the hotel, chess thoughts, chess insomnia and meditations on the drastic defense he had invented to counter Turati's opening. He was wide-awake and his mind worked clearly, purged of all dross and aware that everything apart from chess was only an enchanting dream, in which, like the golden haze of the moon, the image of a sweet, clear-eyed maiden with bare arms dissolved and melted. (*The Defense*, 132–34)

I dreamt of this at night—saw myself fleeing from my grandfather and carrying away with me a toy, or a kitten, or a little crab pressed to my left side. I saw myself meeting poor Lloyd, who appeared to me in my dream hobbling along, hopelessly joined to a hobbling twin while I was free to dance around them and slap them on their humble backs.

I wonder if Lloyd had similar visions. It has been suggested by doctors that we sometimes pooled our minds when we dreamed. One gray-blue morning he picked up a twig and drew a ship with three masts in the dust. I had just seen myself drawing that ship in the dust of a dream I had dreamed the preceding night. ("Scenes from the Life of a Double Monster," *Stories*, 616–17)

Sometimes I attempt to kill in my dreams. But do you know what happens? For instance I hold a gun. For instance I aim at a bland, quietly interested enemy. Oh, I press the trigger all right, but one bullet after another feebly drops on the floor from the sheepish muzzle. In those dreams, my only thought is to conceal the fiasco from my foe, who is slowly growing annoyed. (*Lolita*, 43)

■ *Another almost perfect "Dunne" deal, as this is exactly what happens to Humbert, in surreal terms of his waking life, when he attempts to kill Quilty at least five years later.*

Same date, later, quite late. I have turned on the light to take down a dream. It had an evident antecedent. Haze at dinner had benevolently proclaimed that since the weather bureau promised a sunny weekend we would go to the lake Sunday after church. As I lay in bed, erotically musing before trying to go to sleep, I thought of a final scheme how to profit by the picnic to come. I was aware that mother Haze hated my darling for her being sweet on me. So I planned my lake day with a view to satisfying the mother. To her alone would I talk; but at some appropriate moment I would say I had left my wristwatch or my sunglasses in that glade yonder—and plunge with my nymphet into the wood. Reality at this juncture withdrew, and the Quest for the Glasses turned into a quiet little orgy with a singularly knowing, cheerful, corrupt and compliant Lolita behaving as reason knew she could not possibly behave. At 3 A.M. I swallowed a sleeping pill, and presently, a dream that was not a sequel but a parody revealed to me, with a kind of meaningful clarity, the lake I had never yet visited: it was glazed over with a sheet of emerald ice, and a pockmarked Eskimo was trying in vain to break it with a pickax, although imported mimosas and oleanders flowered on its gravelly banks. I am sure Dr. Blanche Schwarzmann would have paid me a sack of schillings for adding such a libidream to her files. Unfortunately, the rest of it was frankly eclectic. Big Haze and little Haze rode on horseback around the lake, and I rode too, dutifully bobbing up and down, bowlegs astraddle although there was no horse between them, only elastic air—one of those little omissions due to the absentmindedness of the dream agent. (*Lolita*, 49–50)

I could not shake off the feeling of its all being a nightmare that I had had or would have in some other existence, some other sequence of numbered dreams. (*Look at the Harlequins!* 174)

■ *A curious analogue to the dream experiment.*

He stretched, he passed his palms over his <warm> hairy legs, unglued and cupped himself, <with an odd spinning and light-headed sensation> and almost instantly Sleep, with a bow, handed him the key of its city: he understood the meaning of all the lights, <honking> sounds, and <women's gazes> perfumes as everything blended into a single blissful image. Now he seemed to be in a mirrored hall, which wondrously opened on a watery abyss, water glistened in the most unexpected places: he went toward a door past the perfectly credible motorcycle which his landlord was starting with his red heel, and, anticipating indescribable bliss, Franz opened the door and saw Martha standing near the bed <sitting on the edge of the bed>. Eagerly he approached but Tom kept getting in the way; Martha was laughing and shooing away the dog. Now he saw quite closely her glossy lips, her neck swelling with glee, and he too began to hurry, undoing buttons, pulling a blood-stained bone out of the dog's jaws, and feeling an unbearable sweetness welling up within him; he was about to clasp her hips <almost touched her> but suddenly could no longer contain his boiling ecstasy. (*King, Queen, Knave*, 74–75)

Yes, everything about her was excruciating and somehow irremediable, and only in my dreams, drenched with tears, did I at last embrace her and feel under my lips her neck and the hollow near the clavicle. But she would always break away, and I would awaken, still throbbing <sobbing, *vskhlipyvaya* in the original>. . . . Once, at Christmas, before a ball to which they were all going without me, I glimpsed, in a strip of mirror through a door left ajar, her sister powdering Vanya's bare shoulder blades; on another occasion I noticed a flimsy bra in the bathroom. For me these were exhausting events, that had a delicious but dreadfully draining <*sladko,* dulcet, in the original*>* effect on my dreams, although never once in them did I go beyond a hopeless kiss (I myself do not know why I always wept so when we met in my dreams). (*The Eye,* 79–80)

When he had dozed off on the train, he had dreamt a dream grown out of something that Sonia had said. In the dream she pressed his head to her smooth shoulder and bent over him, tickling him with her lips, murmuring warm muffled words of tenderness, and now it was hard to separate fancy from fact. (*Glory,* 119–20)

. . . at night he dreamed of coming across a young girl lying asprawl on a hot lonely beach <*some semi-naked young things on a deserted beach>* and in that dream a sudden fear would seize him of being caught by his wife. (*Laughter in the Dark,* 17)

On the night of the twelfth, he dreamt that he was surreptitiously enjoying Mariette while she sat, wincing a little, in his lap during the rehearsal of a play in which she was supposed to be his daughter. (*Bend Sinister,* 158)

Singularly enough, I seldom if ever dreamed of Lolita as I remembered her—as I saw her constantly and obsessively in my conscious mind during my daymares and insomnias. More precisely: she did haunt my sleep but she appeared there in strange and ludicrous disguises as Valeria or Charlotte, or a cross between them. That complex ghost would come to me, shedding shift after shift, in an atmosphere of great melancholy and disgust, and would recline in dull invitation on some narrow board or hard settee, with flesh ajar like the rubber valve of a soccer ball's bladder. I would bind myself, dentures fractured or hopelessly mislaid, in horrible *chambres garnies* where I would be entertained at tedious vivisecting parties that generally ended with Charlotte or Valeria weeping in my bleeding arms and being tenderly kissed by my brotherly lips in a dream disorder of auctioneered Viennese bric-à-brac, pity, impotence and the brown wigs of tragic old women who had just been gassed. (*Lolita,* 238–39)

The gist, rather than the actual plot of the dream, was a constant refutation of his not loving her. His dreamlove for her exceeded in emotional tone, in spiritual passion and depth, anything he had experienced in his surface existence. This love was like an endless wringing of hands, like a blundering of the soul through an infinite maze of hopelessness and remorse. They were, in a sense, amorous dreams, for they were permeated with tenderness, with a longing to sink his head onto her lap and sob away the monstrous past. They brimmed with the awful awareness of her being so young and so helpless. They were purer than his life. What carnal aura there was in them came not from her but from those with whom he betrayed her—prickly-chinned Phrynia, pretty Timandra with that boom under her apron—and even so the sexual scum remained somewhere far above the sunken treasure and was quite unimportant. (*Pale Fire,* 192)

■ *Novels of the Montreux period contain erotic dreams of the increasingly untender kind that Humbert called "libidreams."*

She moved her head to make him move his to the required angle and her hair touched his neck. In his first dreams of her this re-enacted contact, so light, so brief, invariably proved to be beyond the dreamer's endurance and like a lifted sword signaled fire and violent release. (*Ada,* 39)

He could rely on two or three dreadful dreams to imagine her, in real, or at least responsible, life, recoiling with
a wild look as she left his lust in the lurch to summon her
governess or mother, or a gigantic footman (not existing in
the house but killable in the dream—punchable with sharp-
ringed knuckles, puncturable like a bladder of blood), after
which he knew he would be expelled from Ardis. < . . . >
Next morning, his nose still in the dreambag of a deep pillow
contributed to his otherwise austere bed by sweet Blanche
(with whom, by the parlor-game rules of sleep, he had been
holding hands in a heartbreaking nightmare—or perhaps it
was just her cheap perfume), the boy was at once aware of the
happiness knocking to be let in. He deliberately endeavored
to prolong the glow of its incognito by dwelling on the last
vestiges of jasmine and tears in a silly dream; but the tiger of
happiness fairly leaped into being. (*Ada*, 97)

That night, in a post-Moët dream, he sat on the talc of a trop-
ical beach full of sun-baskers, and one moment was rubbing
the red, irritated shaft of a writhing boy, and the next was
looking through dark glasses at the symmetrical shading on
either side of a shining spine with fainter shading between
the ribs belonging to Lucette or Ada sitting on a towel at
some distance from him. Presently, she turned and lay prone,
and she, too, wore sunglasses, and neither he nor she could
perceive the exact direction of each other's gaze through the
black amber, yet he knew by the dimple of a faint smile that
she was looking at his (it had been his all the time) raw scarlet. (*Ada,* 520–21)

Person, *this* person, was on the imagined brink of imagined
bliss when Armande's footfalls approached—striking out
both "imagined" in the proof's margin (never too wide for
corrections and queries!). (*Transparent Things,* 102)

Recurrent, Fatidic

I have noticed, or seem to have noticed, in the course of my long life, that when about to fall in love or even when still unaware of having fallen in love, a dream would come, introducing me to a latent inamorata at morning twilight in a somewhat infantile setting, marked by exquisite aching stirrings that I knew as a boy, as a youth, as a madman, as an old dying voluptuary. The sense of recurrence ("seem to have noticed") is very possibly a built-in feeling: for instance I may have had that dream only once or twice ("in the course of my long life") and its familiarity is only the dropper that comes with the drops. The place in the dream, per contra, is not a familiar room but one remindful of the kind we children awake in after a Christmas masquerade or midsummer name day, in a great house, belonging to strangers or distant cousins. The impression is that the beds, two small beds in the present case, have been put in and placed against the opposite walls of a room that is not a bedroom at heart, a room with no furniture except those two separate beds: property masters are lazy, or economical, in one's dreams as well as in early novellas. In one of the beds I find myself just awoken from some secondary dream of only formulary importance; and in the far bed against the right-hand wall (direction also supplied), a girl, a younger, slighter, and gayer Annette in this particular variant (summer of 1934 by daytime reckoning), is playfully, quietly talking to herself but actually, as I understand with a delicious quickening of the nether pulses, is feigning to talk, is talking for my benefit, so as to be noticed by me. My next thought—and it intensifies the throbbings—concerns the strangeness of boy and girl being assigned to sleep in the same makeshift room: by error, no doubt, or perhaps the house was full and the distance between the two beds, across an empty floor, might have been deemed wide enough for perfect decorum in the case of children (my average age has been thirteen all my life). The cup of pleasure is brimming by now and before it spills I hasten to tiptoe across the bare parquet from my bed to hers. Her fair hair gets in the way of my kisses, but presently my lips find her cheek and neck, and her nightgown has buttons, and she says the maid has come into the room, but it is too late, I cannot restrain myself, and the maid, a beauty in her own right, looks on, laughing.

That dream I had a month or so after I met Annette, and her image in it, that early version of her voice, soft hair, tender skin, obsessed me and amazed me with delight—the delight of discovering I loved little Miss Blagovo. (*Look at the Harlequins!* 101–3)

My sexual life is virtually over but—I saw you again, Aurora Lee, whom as a youth I had pursued with hopeless desire at high-school balls—and whom I have cornered now fifty years later, on a terrace of my dream. Your painted pout and cold gaze were, come to think of it, very like the official lips and eyes of Flora, my wayward wife, and your flimsy frock of black silk might have come from her recent wardrobe. You turned away, but could not escape, trapped as you were among the close-set columns of moonlight and I lifted the hem of your dress—something I never had done in the past—and stroked, moulded, pinched ever so softly your pale prominent nates, while you stood perfectly still as if considering new possibilities of power and pleasure and interior decoration. At the height of your guarded ecstasy I thrust my cupped hand from behind between your consenting thighs and felt the sweat-stuck folds of a long scrotum and then, further in front, the droop of a short member. Speaking as an authority on dreams, I wish to add that this was no homosexual manifestation but a splendid example of terminal gynandrism.

Young Aurora Lee (who was to be axed and chopped up at seventeen by an idiot lover, all glasses and beard) and half-impotent old Wild formed for a moment one creature. But quite apart from all that, in a more disgusting and delicious sense, her little bottom, so smooth, so moonlit, a replica, in fact, of her twin brother's charms (sampled rather brutally on my last night at boarding school), remained inset in the medallion of every following day. (*The Original of Laura*, 201–7)

NESTED

This occurs not infrequently: You come to, and see yourself, say, sitting in an elegant second-class compartment with a couple of elegant strangers; actually, though, this is a false awakening, being merely the next layer of your dream, as if you were rising up from stratum to stratum but never reaching the surface, never emerging into reality. Your spellbound thought, however, mistakes every new layer of the dream for the door of reality. (*King, Queen, Knave*, 20)

I dreamed a loathsome dream, a triple ephialtes. First there was a small dog; but not simply a small dog; a small mock dog, very small, with the minute black eyes of a beetle's larva; it was white through and through, and coldish. Flesh? No, not flesh, but rather grease or jelly, or else perhaps, the fat of a white worm, with, moreover, a kind of carved corrugated surface reminding one of a Russian paschal lamb of butter— disgusting mimicry. A cold-blooded being, which Nature had twisted into the likeness of a small dog with a tail and legs, all as it should be. It kept getting into my way, I could not avoid it; and when it touched me, I felt something like an electric shock. I woke up. On the sheet of the bed next to mine there lay curled up, like a swooned white larva, that very same dreadful little pseudo dog. . . . I groaned with disgust and opened my eyes. All around shadows floated; the bed next to mine was empty except for the broad burdock leaves which, owing to the damp, grow out of bedsteads. One could see, on those leaves, telltale stains of a slimy nature; I peered closer; there, glued to a fat stem it sat, small, tallowish-white, with its little black button eyes . . . but then, at last, I woke up for good. (*Despair*, 106–7)

And presently he found out that he could not live without her, and presently she found out that she had had quite enough of hearing him talk of his dreams, and the dreams in his dreams, and the dreams in the dreams of his dreams. (*The Real Life of Sebastian Knight*, 159)

He had spent most of the day fast asleep in his room, and a long, rambling, dreary dream had repeated, in a kind of pointless parody, his strenuous "Casanovanic" night with Ada and that somehow ominous morning talk with her. Now that I am writing this, after so many hollows and heights of time, I find it not easy to separate our conversation, as set down in an inevitably stylized form, and the drone of complaints, turning on sordid betrayals that obsessed young Van in his dull nightmare. Or was he dreaming now that he had been dreaming? (*Ada*, 198)

He heard Ada Vinelander's voice calling for her Glass bed slippers (which, as in Cordulenka's princessdom too, he found hard to distinguish from dance footwear), and a minute later, without the least interruption in the established tension, Van found himself, in a drunken dream, making violent love to Rose—no, to Ada, but in the rosacean fashion, on a kind of lowboy. She complained he hurt her "like a Tiger Turk." He went to bed and was about to doze off for good when she left his side. (*Ada*, 415–16)

He dreamed that he was speaking in the lecturing hall of a transatlantic liner and that a bum resembling the hitch-hiker from Hilden was asking sneeringly how did the lecturer explain that in our dreams we know we shall awake, is not that analogous to the certainty of death and if so, the future—(*Ada,* 561)

LIFE IS A DREAM

■ *This ancient notion, which gave the title to Calderón's famous play, and its logical extension (death is awakening), are assayed in a number of Nabokov's fictions, most directly in* Invitation to a Beheading.

By an implacable repetition of moves it was leading once more to that same passion which would destroy the dream of life. Devastation, horror, madness. (*The Defense,* 246)

It is frightening when real life suddenly turns out to be a dream, but how much more frightening when that which one had thought a dream—fluid and irresponsible—suddenly starts to congeal into reality! (*The Eye,* 106)

Strange: all dread had gone. The nightmare had melted into the keen, sweet sensation of absolute freedom, peculiar to sinful dreams. (*Laughter in the Dark,* 66–67)

■ *The original continues: "for life is a dream" (omitted in the English version).*

Maybe it is all mock existence, an evil dream; and presently I shall wake up somewhere; on a patch of grass near Prague. A good thing, at least, that they brought me to bay so speedily. (*Despair,* 221)

And yet, ever since early childhood, I have had dreams. . . . In my dreams the world was ennobled, spiritualized; people whom in the waking state I feared so much appeared there in a shimmering refraction, just as if they were imbued with and enveloped by that vibration of light which in sultry weather inspires the very outlines of objects with life; their voices, their step, the expressions of their eyes and even of their clothes—acquired an exciting significance; to put it more simply, in my dreams the world would come alive, becoming so captivatingly majestic, free and ethereal, that afterwards it would be oppressive to breathe the dust of this painted life. But then I have long since grown accustomed to the thought that what we call dreams is semi-reality, the promise of reality, a foreglimpse and a whiff of it; that is, they contain, in a very vague, diluted state, more genuine reality than our vaunted waking life which, in its turn, is semi-sleep, an evil drowsiness into which penetrate in grotesque disguise the sounds and sights of the real world, flowing beyond the periphery of the mind—as when you hear during sleep a dreadful insidious tale because a branch is scraping on the pane, or see yourself sinking into snow because your blanket is sliding off. But how I fear awakening! (*Invitation to a Beheading,* 91–92)

ONEIRIC REALISM

■ *Fantastic imagery appearing deceptively real and utterly believable. Nabokov often invokes the notion of a dream director responsible for these grotesque shows, with a self-suggesting analogy of fiction-writing.*

A sophisticated dreamer (for to see dreams is an art form in its own right), he most often had the following dream . . . (*Camera Obscura,* 96). <*The description of the dream that follows is markedly different from the English version below, more elaborate and plausible: the Russian Horn (renamed Rex in English) gets four aces one after the other, then draws a joker. The English text goes:>*

Having cultivated a penchant for bluff since his tenderest age, no wonder his favorite card-game was poker! He played it whenever he could get partners; and he played it in his dreams: with historical characters or some distant cousin of his, long dead, whom in real life he never remembered, or with people who—in real life again—would have flatly refused to be in the same room with him. In that dream he took up, stacked together, and lifted close to his eyes the five dealt to him, saw with pleasure the joker in cap and bells, and, as he pressed out with a cautious thumb one top corner and then another, he found by degrees that he had five jokers. "Excellent," he thought to himself, without any surprise at their plurality, and quietly made his first bet, which Henry the Eighth (by Holbein) who had only four queens, doubled. Then he woke up, still with his poker face. (*Laughter in the Dark,* 141)

It was all very nice, very prim at that party. We talked about things that did not concern him, and I knew that if I mentioned his name there would flash in the eyes of each of them the same sacerdotal alarm. And when I suddenly found myself wearing a suit cut by my neighbor on the right, and eating my vis-à-vis' pastry, which I washed down with a special kind of mineral water prescribed by my neighbor on the left, I was overcome by a dreadful, dream-significant feeling, which immediately awakened me—in my poor-man's room, with a poor-man's moon in the curtainless window. I am grateful to the night for even such a dream: of late I have been racked by insomnia. It is as if his agents were accustoming me beforehand to the most popular of the tortures inflicted on present-day criminals. ("Tyrants Destroyed," *Stories,* 449)

And the dream I had: that garlicky doctor (who was at the same time Falter, or was it Alexander Vasilievich?) replying with exceptional readiness, that yes, of course it sometimes did happen, and that such children (i.e., the posthumously born) were known as cadaverkins. As to you, never once since you died have you appeared in my dreams. Perhaps the authorities intercept you, or you yourself avoid such prison visits with me. ("Ultima Thule," *Stories*, 501–2)

I remember once dreaming of her: I dreamt that my eldest girl had run in to tell me the doorman was sorely in trouble—and when I had gone down to him, I saw lying on a trunk, a roll of burlap under her head, pale-lipped and wrapped in a woolen kerchief, Nina fast asleep, as miserable refugees sleep in godforsaken railway stations. ("Spring in Fialta," *Stories*, 425)

Now he found himself running (by night, ugly? Yah, by night, folks) down something that looked like a railway track through a long damp tunnel (the dream stage management having used the first set available for rendering 'tunnel,' without bothering to remove either the rails or the ruby lamps that glowed at intervals along the rocky black sweating walls). (*Bend Sinister*, 58)

On the eve of the day fixed by Quist he found himself on the bridge: he was out reconnoitring, since it had occurred to him that as a meeting place it might be unsafe because of the soldiers; but the soldiers had gone long ago, the bridge was deserted, Quist could come whenever he liked. Krug had only one glove, and he had forgotten his glasses, so could not reread the careful note Quist had given him with all the passwords and addresses and a sketch map and the key to the code of Krug's whole life. It mattered little however. The sky immediately overhead was quilted with a livid and billowy expanse of thick cloud; very large, greyish, semitransparent, irregularly shaped snowflakes slowly and vertically descended; and when they touched the dark water of the Kur, they floated upon it instead of melting at once, and this was strange. Further on, beyond the edge of the cloud; a sudden nakedness of heaven and river smiled at the bridge-bound observer, and a mother-of-pearl radiance touched up the curves of the remote mountains, from which the river, and the smiling sadness, and the first evening lights in the windows of riverside buildings were variously derived. Watching the snowflakes upon the dark and beautiful water, Krug argued that either the flakes were real, and the water was not real water, or else the latter was real, whereas the flakes were made of some special insoluble stuff. In order to settle the question, he let his mateless glove fall from the bridge; but nothing abnormal happened: the glove simply pierced the corrugated surface of the water with its extended index, dived and was gone.

On the south bank (from which he had come) he could see, further upstream, Paduk's pink palace and the bronze dome of the Cathedral, and the leafless trees of a public garden. On the other side of the river there were rows of old tenement houses beyond which (unseen but throbbingly present) stood the hospital where she had died. As he brooded thus, sitting sideways on a stone bench and looking at the river, a tugboat dragging a barge appeared in the distance and at the same time one of the last snowflakes (the cloud overhead seemed to be dissolving in the now generously flushed sky) grazed his underlip: it was a regular soft wet flake, he reflected, but perhaps those that had been descending upon the water itself had been different ones. The tug steadily approached. As it was about to plunge under the bridge, the great black funnel, doubly encircled with crimson, was pulled back, back and down by two men clutching at its rope and grinning with sheer exertion; one of them was a Chinese as were most of the river people and washermen of the town. On the barge behind, half a dozen brightly coloured shirts were drying and some potted geraniums could be seen aft, and a very fat Olga in the yellow blouse he disliked, arms akimbo, looked up at Krug as the barge in its turn was smoothly engulfed by the arch of the bridge.

He awoke (asprawl in his leather armchair) and immediately understood that something extraordinary had happened. It had nothing to do with the dream or the quite unprovoked and rather ridiculous physical discomfort he felt (a local congestion) or anything that he recalled in connection with the appearance of his room (untidy and dusty in an untidy and dusty light) or the time of the day (a quarter past eight p.m.; he had fallen asleep after an early supper). What had happened was that again he knew he could write. (*Bend Sinister*, 168–70)

He had fallen asleep at last, despite the discomfort in his back, and in the course of one of those dreams that still haunt Russian fugitives, even when a third of a century has elapsed since their escape from the Bolsheviks, Pnin saw himself fantastically cloaked, fleeing through great pools of ink under a cloud-barred moon from a chimerical palace, and then pacing a desolate strand with his dead friend Ilya Isidorovich Polyanski as they waited for some mysterious deliverance to arrive in a throbbing boat from beyond the hopeless sea. (*Pnin*, 109–10)

That exhilaration of a newly acquired franchise! A shade of it he seemed to have kept in his sleep, in that last part of his recent dream in which he had told Blanche that he had learned to levitate and that his ability to treat air with magic ease would allow him to break all records for the long jump by strolling, as it were, a few inches above the ground for a stretch of say thirty or forty feet (too great a length might be suspicious) while the stands went wild, and Zambovsky of Zambia stared, arms akimbo, in consternation and disbelief. (*Ada*, 123)

FATHER

■ *Seeing one's dead father in a dream is a particularly poignant theme in Nabokov's fiction.*

That night Mark had an unpleasant dream. He saw his late father. His father came up to him, with an odd smile on his pale, sweaty face, seized Mark under the arms, and began to tickle him silently, violently, and relentlessly. He only remembered that dream after he had arrived at the store where he worked, and he remembered it because a friend of his, jolly Adolf, poked him in the ribs. For one instant something flew open in his soul, momentarily froze still in surprise, and slammed shut. ("Details of a Sunset," *Stories*, 81).

He went to bed and began to fall asleep to the whisper of the rain. As always on the border between consciousness and sleep all sorts of verbal rejects, sparkling and tinkling, broke in: "The crystal crunching of that Christian night beneath a chrysolitic star" . . . and his thought, listening for a moment, aspired to gather them and use them and began to add of its own: Extinguished, Yasnaya Polyana's light, and Pushkin dead, and Russia far . . . but since this was no good, the stipple of rhymes extended further: "A falling star, a cruising chrysolite, an aviator's avatar . . ." His mind sank lower and lower into a hell of alligator alliterations, into infernal cooperatives of words. Through their nonsensical accumulation a round button on the pillowcase prodded him in the cheek; he turned on his other side and against a dark backdrop naked people ran into the Grunewald lake, and a monogram of light resembling an infusorian glided diagonally to the highest corner of his subpal-pebral field of vision. Behind a certain closed door in his brain, holding on to its handle but turning away from it, his mind commenced to discuss with somebody a complicated and important secret, but when the door opened for a minute it turned out that they were talking about chairs, tables, stables. Suddenly in the thickening mist, by reason's last tollgate, came the silver vibration of a telephone bell, and Fyodor rolled over prone, falling. . . . The vibration stayed in his fingers, as if a nettle had stung him. In the hall, having already put back the receiver into its black box, stood Zina—she seemed frightened. "That was for you," she said in a low voice. "Your former landlady, Frau Stoboy. She wants you to come over immediately. There's somebody waiting for you at her place. Hurry." He pulled on a pair of flannel trousers and gasping for breath went along the street. At this time of year in Berlin there is something similar to the St. Petersburg white nights: the air was transparently gray, and the houses swam past like a soapy mirage. Some night workers had wrecked the pavement at the corner, and one had to creep through narrow passages between planks, everyone being given at the entrance a small lamp which at the exit was to be left on a hook screwed into a post or else simply on the sidewalk next to some empty milk bottles. Leaving his bottle as well he ran further through the lusterless streets, and the premonition of something incredible, of some impossible superhuman surprise splashed his heart with a snowy mixture of happiness and horror. In the gray murk, blind children wearing dark spectacles came out of a school building in pairs and walked past him; they studied at night (in economically dark schools which in the daytime housed

seeing children), and the clergyman accompanying them resembled the Leshino village schoolmaster, Bychkov. Leaning
against a lamppost and hanging his tousled head, his scissor-
like legs in striped pantaloons splayed wide and his hands
stuffed in his pockets, a lean drunkard stood as if just come
from the pages of an old Russian satirical rag. There was still
light in the Russian bookstore—they were serving books to
the night taxi-cab drivers and through the yellow opacity of
the glass he noticed the silhouette of Misha Berezovski who
was handing out Petrie's black atlas to someone. Must be
hard to work nights! Excitement lashed him again as soon as
he reached his former haunts. He was out of breath from
running, and the rolled-up laprobe weighed heavy on his
arm—he had to hurry, but he could not recall the layout of
the streets, and the ashy night confused everything, changing
as in a negative image the relationship between dark and
light parts, and there was no one to ask, everybody was
asleep. Suddenly a poplar loomed and behind it a tall church
with a violet-red window divided into harlequin rhombuses
of colored light: inside a night service was in progress, and an
old lady in mourning with cotton-wool under the bridge of
her spectacles hastened to mount the steps. He found his
street, but at the end of it a post with a gauntleted hand on it
indicated that one had to enter from the other end where the
post office was, since at this end a pile of flags had been prepared for tomorrow's festivities. But he was afraid of losing it
in the course of a detour and moreover the post office—that
would come afterwards—if Mother had not *already* been sent
a telegram. He scrambled over boards, boxes and a toy gren-
adier in curls, and caught sight of the familiar house, and
there the workmen had already stretched a red strip of carpet
across the sidewalk from door to curb, as it used to be done
in front of their house on the Neva Embankment on ball
nights. He ran up the stairs and Frau Stoboy immediately let

him in. Her cheeks glowed and she wore a white hospital overall—she had formerly practiced medicine. "Only don't get all worked up," she said. "Go to your room and wait there. You must be prepared for anything," she added with a vibrant note in her voice and pushed him into the room which he had thought he would never in his life enter again. He grasped her by the elbow, losing control over himself, but she shook him off. "Somebody has come to see you," said Stoboy, "he's resting. . . . Wait a couple of minutes." The door banged shut. The room was exactly as if he had been still living in it: the same swans and lilies on the wallpaper, the same painted ceiling wonderfully ornamented with Tibetan butterflies (there, for example, was *Thecla bieti*). Expectancy, awe, the frost of happiness, the surge of sobs merged into a single blinding agitation as he stood in the middle of the room incapable of movement, listening and looking at the door. He knew *who* would enter in a moment, and was amazed now that he had doubted this return: doubt now seemed to him to be the obtuse obstinacy of one half-witted, the distrust of a barbarian, the self-satisfaction of an ignoramus. His heart was bursting like that of a man before execution, but at the same time this execution was such a joy that life faded before it, and he was unable to understand the disgust he had been wont to experience when, in hastily constructed dreams, he had evoked what was now taking place in real life. Suddenly, the door shuddered (another, remote one had opened somewhere beyond it) and he heard a familiar tread, an indoor Morocco-padded step. Noiselessly but with terrible force the door flew open, and on the threshold stood his father. He was wearing a gold embroidered skullcap and a black Cheviot jacket with breast pockets for cigarette case and magnifying glass; his brown cheeks with their two sharp furrows running down from both sides of his nose were particularly smoothly shaven; hoary hairs gleamed in his dark beard like salt; warmly, shaggily, his eyes laughed out of a network of wrinkles. But Fyodor stood and was unable to take a step. His father said something, but so quietly that it was impossible to make anything out, although one somehow knew it to be connected with his return, unharmed, whole, human, and real. And even so it was terrible to come closer—so terrible that Fyodor felt he would die if the one who had entered should move toward him. Somewhere in the rear rooms sounded the warningly rapturous laughter of his mother, while his father made soft chucking sounds hardly parting his lips, as he used to do when taking a decision or seeking something on the page of a book . . . then he spoke again—and this again meant that everything was all right and simple, that this was the true resurrection, that it could not be otherwise, and also: that he was pleased—pleased with his captures, his return, his son's book about him—and then at last everything grew easy, a light broke through, and his father with confident joy spread out his arms. With a moan and a sob Fyodor stepped toward him, and in the collective sensation of woolen jacket, big hands and the tender prickle of trimmed mustaches there swelled an ecstatically happy, living, enormous, paradisal warmth in which his icy heart melted and dissolved.

At first the superposition of a thingummy on a thingabob and the pale, palpitating stripe that went upwards were utterly incomprehensible, like words in a forgotten language or the parts of a dismantled engine—and this senseless tangle sent a shiver of panic running through him: I have woken up in the grave, on the moon, in the dungeon of dingy nonbeing. But something in his brain turned, his thoughts settled and hastened to paint over the truth—and he realized that he was looking at the curtain of a half-open window, at a table in front of the window: such is the treaty with reason—the theater of earthly habit, the livery of temporary substance. He lowered his head onto the pillow and tried to overtake a fugitive sense—warm, wonderful, all-explaining—but the new dream he dreamt was an uninspired compilation, stitched together out of remnants of daytime life and fitted to it. (*The Gift*, 363–67).

■ *It is instructive to read this masterful passage alongside Nabokov's diary entry fresh after his father's assassination: see Boyd,* Russian Years, *191–93, and Pitzer,* Secret History, *75.*

INSOMNIA

Well—on that terrible day when, devastated by a sleepless night, I stepped out into the center of an incidental city, and saw houses, trees, automobiles, people, my mind abruptly refused to accept them as "houses," "trees," and so forth—as something connected with ordinary human life. My line of communication with the world snapped, I was on my own and the world was on its own, and that world was devoid of sense. ("Terror," *Stories*, 176–77)

My nerves were unusually receptive after a sleepless night; I assimilated everything: the whistling of a thrush in the almond trees beyond the chapel, the peace of the crumbling houses, the pulse of the distant sea, panting in the mist, all this together with the jealous green of bottle glass bristling along the top of a wall and the fast colors of a circus advertisement featuring a feathered Indian on a rearing horse in the act of lassoing a boldly endemic zebra, while some thoroughly fooled elephants sat brooding upon their star-spangled thrones. ("Spring in Fialta," *Stories*, 414)

PART 5

ARTISTIC TIME

TWO PRIME MYSTERIES

*And when you look over the railing at the bubbly foam rapidly
running away, you feel as if you were drifting further and
further backwards, standing on the very stern of Time.*

—Other Shores[1]

ALL HIS CONSCIOUS LIFE Nabokov was pondering the chief
structuring condition of earthly existence, Time. Death, the
borderline demarcated by the pale fire of uncreated light
beyond which time should be no longer,[2] was a mystery
whose magnetic chill he felt almost from the "cradle rocking
above an abyss."[3] It is possible to consider his drive to write
fiction as a sustained attempt at various inquiries into the
carefully prepared conditions of time and space. The English
term "novel," a secondhand Italian import, is feckless (as is
much of the English generic literary terminology) because it
is completely unattached to the drivetrain of the genre, without which, or with an unskilled handling of which, it reliably
fails. That drivetrain is Time; that is what sets a "romance,"
to use another unfortunate term, apart from other genres of
prose fiction.

1. My translation.
2. Rev. 10:6.
3. From the opening sentence of Nabokov's memoirs.

Proper time handling requires room—and not the other way round: the cardinal difference between a "short story" and a "novel" is not that the latter is a "long story" but that there are specific space demands for re-creating timeflow plausibly. Time in fiction is not mere chronology that ought to be monitored. It is rather a most difficult, deliberate verbal production of the effects of time passing, jumping, bucking, crawling, elapsing, warping, forking, reversing that we experience but can never quite get accustomed to in the course of life. A better term for a "novel" would be something like *chronopoeia*, a time-craft in writing, compositional time-management, the taming of time.

All Nabokov's novels are masterfully chronopoetic. He studied in detail, valued highly, and presented to his Cornell students aspects of this very special branch of craftsmanship in Proust, who deftly managed temporal springs and neaps; in Tolstoy, who somehow synchronized his tweaked, thirty-six-hour-a-day chronometer with the mesmerized reader's standard watch; in Joyce, who broke a score of hours of a single day into twelve-hundred elastic minutes. And, as said before, Nabokov's own composing of "long fiction" may be viewed as an extended, specialized experiment with Time whose ultimate goal was, if not to grasp then at least to touch the enigma of mortality—a highly pleasurable means to a wittingly unattainable end.

On February 14, 1951, he wrote in his diary:

Space, time, the two prime mysteries. The transformation of nothing into something cannot be conceived by the human mind.

Revisiting the entry on the same date eight years later he added:

The torrent of time—a mere poetical tradition: time does not flow. Time is perfectly still. We feel it as moving only because it is the medium where growth and change take place or where things stop, like stations.

Two days later he drafted a clear-cut supposition that he had tried in less streamlined forms in his earlier writing and that became a founding principle in his last three novels:

Feb. 16.

From the point of view of evolutionary dialectics the hereafter finds its beautiful proof in the following series:

1. Time without consciousness (the lower animal world)
2. Time with consciousness (man = *chelovek*[4] = conscious Time)
3. Consciousness without Time (the future of the immortal soul)

The last term is really the thesis of a new series.[5]

It can be said, perhaps, that before his "experiment with time" according to Dunne's prescription, Nabokov's view of the place of time in art was somewhat simplistic: he proposed that art depended on the "perfect fusion of the past and the present," but "the inspiration of genius adds a third ingredient: it is the past and the present and the future (your book) that come together in a sudden flash; thus the entire circle of time is perceived, which is another way of saying that time ceases to exist."[6] This position grew much more sophisticated by the 1960s, after the experiment—arguably, as a result of it.

4. Russian for "man."
5. Berg Collection, Manuscript Box: "Diaries, 1951–1959."
6. *Lectures*, 378.

Thaw, snow almost gone except for
strange, bird-like, penguin-like remnants
(~~fate~~ due to the incomplete action of snowplow blades
~~the old act of the snow roadity flow~~)
lined up, greyish with dark heads
along curbs, on the raised side walk side.

From the point of view of evolutionary
dialectics the hereafter finds its beautiful
proof in the following series :
1. Time without consciousness (the
       lower animal world)
2. Time with consciousness (man =
       <u>ZERO</u>BEK = Conscious Time)
3. Consciousness without Time
       (the future of the immortal soul)

   ~~soul~~
The last term is ~~merely~~ really
the thesis of a new series.

THE MONTREUX NOVELS

Rightly heard, all tales are one.

—Cormac McCarthy[7]

Nabokov's post-experiment fiction—three published novels and one left unfinished at the time of his death, all written inside and in the vicinity of a Swiss grand hotel in Montreux, where he lived for the last fifteen years of his life—differed from his previous novels in a number of ways. The most significant difference is a new and special handling of the time dimension, that "backbone of consciousness," as Van Veen puts it, and therefore the backbone of any artistic fiction simulating the human condition. Time-travel became much more extended than before, making up, in a disproportionately staggered form, the entirety of *Ada* and much of the other two novels' narrative space.

Time-molding took very complex shapes. Death, as a personal end of time, grew into an overarching theme. In all these novels Nabokov seems to be testing Dunne's idea that Time is not an inexorable, irreversible Heraclitic river-stream that cannot be entered twice and so on; rather, it is an alternating electric current that pulses in both directions. Change can be changed back.

The cards on which he drafted *Ada*, the first fiction Nabokov wrote after his dream experiment, shared a big folder with the dream cards. The seven-year gap between that novel and the previous, *Pale Fire*, was the longest for him,[8] and the resulting book turned out to be twice as fat as the previous largest, *The Gift*. Like that Russian novel, *Ada* is made up of five parts; unlike it, the parts are of pointedly unequal length. Part 4 is the plot-carrying core: most of its room

---

7. *The Crossing*, 406.

8. Eight years separate the publication of *Bend Sinister* and *Lolita*, but there was a book of memoir, a nonfiction novel, right in between.

is taken by Van Veen's essay entitled *The Texture of Time*. Its postulate is basically apophatic: the notion of Time should not be confused with, or suffused by, that of space: the two must be uncoupled once and for all. Yet within the novel this proposition contains a curious self-biting antinomy: Van is mind-handling this theory while driving at full throttle to meet Ada at Mont Roux, as if ignoring the fact that speed is time mating distance (and he somehow erases a day in the process).[9] In a remarkable scene in *The Gift*, a character lying in bed in a darkened room, pondering death, hears the noise of "trickling and drumming" water behind the tightly blinded window and arrives at the trite conclusion that there is nothing *afterward*, which, he thinks, is as certain as the fact that it is raining. And yet it is bright and sunny outside, and the tenant upstairs is watering her flowers on the balcony. Could Van's conviction that time and space must be divorced be similarly mistaken? After all, the morning after that spastic journey through space, in a frantic effort to outrun time, he sees, against all expectations, Ada standing on the balcony one floor below his.

Nabokov, who once let it be understood that he did not share all of Van's views on time,[10] seems to undermine the cardinal point of Van's theory by correlating temporal dimension with a spatial one. *Ada*'s five parts are sized in inverse proportion to the time period they span. "Time is rhythm," pronounces Van;[11] but rhythm is the spacing of time. Part 1, composed of 43 chapters, takes up 325 pages in the first edition, well over half of the book's total bulk, and covers the events of less than four years, 1884 to 1888 (discounting the pluperfects at the beginning

---

9. See Dieter Zimmer's most useful "*Ada*'s Timeline" at dezimmer.net. Van drives flat-out, but he twice takes the wrong turn, has to make up time—and one day gets skipped.
10. *Strong Opinions*, 143.
11. *Ada*, 537.

necessary to flesh out Van and Ada's common genealogy); part 2, of only 11 chapters and 120 pages, propels the narration to 1893; part 3 has eight chapters and 93 pages but covers 29 years, 1893 to 1922. The seminal part 4 makes up a single harried chapter and spans, in a matter of 28 brisk pages, the three (or four) days in mid-July 1922. (It is the only part with no interpolations by Ada, who nevertheless has the last word: "We can know the time, we can know a time. We can never know Time. Our senses are simply not meant to perceive it. It is like—" . . . death was probably the inaudible word, or what comes after death.) Van Veen covers considerable space in a relatively short time, all the while trying to cut off Time from "Siamese Space" and to expound on the falsehood of the future—which comes rushing in the last part, only 22 pages long, its hurried six chapters accounting for the rest of the timeline, a tremendous space of 45 years. There is a neat stability in this receding proportion: the size ratio of parts that have one part between them (I–III, II–IV, and III–V) is kept about the same: four to one. In a sense, this inversely progressive despacing is akin to the phenomenon of the reverse perspective, a concept that Florensky explored in depth in 1919–24.[12]

Viewed another way, Nabokov uses about 30,000 words to present one year for the first four years of narration (including the initial flashbacks); about 9,000 words per year for the five following; approximately 1,200 words per year on average for the next 29; and allots only about 400 per year for the remaining 45 years of the storyline, counting parts 4 and 5 together. "Time is but memory in the making,"[13] Van states further, and his chronicle drives the point home, so to speak, since the first four years are more richly worded,

12. See Florensky-1999, 46–103, and Florensky-2000, 190–258. The term "umgekehrte Perspektive" as related to artwork was suggested by Oskar Wulff in a 1907 essay.

13. *Ada*, 559.

much more brightly preserved, much better restored, in other words, much more real than the remaining eighty, getting dimmer as Van and Ada asymptotically get older.

His next novel, *Transparent Things*, is half the size of *Ada*'s part 1 alone. Its intricate diegetic device removes the bodiless narrators, all of them dead, from terrestrial conditions and places those spirits in the timeless realm from which they unfold the story of Hugh Person. They pronounce utterances in unison, like a tragic chorus; they know in depth the past and in width the present of all men and things, and the future for them is, presumably, the present. This design is so difficult that, seeing that even the sharpest readers did not quite grasp it, Nabokov went so far as to make up an interview in which he explains to the imaginary questioner the book's real plot-work.[14] It is of note that the title is a double-take, of the *Finnegans Wake* type: the narrating "things" are transparent (invisible) to the living; at the same time, all things are transparent (knowable) to them. Incidentally, since both these aspects cannot be retained in one Russian phrase (because the stricter semantic range of the word "things" drains the phrase of the first meaning), Nabokov privately called this slim but significant book in Russian *Skvozniak iz proshlago*, a draught from the past, a line from his 1930 poem about a sense of the hereafter, entitled "To the Future Reader."[15] This arrangement is markedly different from the way Dante's spirits see the time dimension: the past and the future are indeed transparent to them, but they are "denied the sight of present things."[16]

14. Collected in *Strong Opinions,* which apparently contains two more auto-interviews.

15. Related to the author by Nabokov's widow in a private conversation.

16. "It seems, if I hear right, that you can see
   beforehand that which time is carrying,
   but you're denied the sight of present things."
   "We see, even as men who are farsighted,
   those things," he said, "that are remote from us;

Like Van Veen, Vadim Vadimych N., the narrator of the last novel Nabokov published, rather senses than suspects the coexistence of another world, unreachable but permeable, which his much happier and healthier maker inhabits. Is his world an interminable dream? One of Dunne's important points is that precognitive dreaming is a normal human faculty, which almost nobody registers owing to inattention. VVN is beset by what he thinks is a singular mental handicap, perhaps a sign of encroaching madness: he cannot perform a mental roundabout of spatial progress so that he would see objects just passed in reverse order. As if confirming Van's insistence on removing Space from the space-time, VVN's marvelously congenial last wife resolves his lifelong conundrum by explaining that he takes imagined spatial progress for temporal: it is exceedingly hard to reverse Time. Yet memory does not reverse it: it makes the past present.

BOOMERANGING TIME

It's queer, I seem to remember my future works, although I don't even know what they will be about.
—The Gift[17]

Definitions of Time usually exhibit a tendency toward short-circuiting. A character in a mimetic fiction may be allowed to conceive time as rhythm or as memory-in-the-making, but he cannot have license to imagine a world transcendental to his

---

the Highest Lord allots us that much light.
But when events draw near or are, our minds
are useless; were we not informed by others,
we should know nothing of your human state.
So you can understand how our awareness
will die completely at the moment when
the portal of the future has been shut."
—*Inferno* 10: 97–108 (*trans. Allen Mandelbaum*)
17. First imaginary dialogue.

in which his time could be stretched, kneaded, or reversed as need be, that is, in effect a world where, from his standpoint, there is no time. Van Veen might feel at home in the company of the so-called detensers, such as J. M. McTaggart and, to a lesser degree, his younger Cambridge colleague and opponent Bertrand Russell, who tried to divorce Time not only from Space but also from itself, collapsing the dimension to a figure of speech. If Time is an allegory for change, then, they would argue, change is "nothing more than things having different properties at different times."[18]

It is not unthinkable, though rather unlikely, that Nabokov saw an interesting 1935 letter to the editor of *Philosophy*, a quarterly published by Cambridge University, in regard to Dunne's theory of Time. While conceding that "general indebtedness of thought to Dunne" may be great, Joshua Gregory, a British philosopher of considerable renown, a younger colleague of McTaggart and Russell, arrives at a conclusion very similar to Van Veen's: "[The] presumed infinite regress of Time is based fallaciously on an illegitimate spatialization," pointing out a "seeming initial error—an attempt to convert Time into a kind of Space."[19] And yet the measuring rod of astrophysicists is the distance that light covers in a year: an exemplary space-in-time unit.

Modern physical science is so thoroughly alienated from metaphysics, indeed from any sort of idealistic philosophy, that attempts to make sense of the relationship between quantum mechanics and gravitational theory lead to dry absurdities, because, in the shrewd words of a recent interpreter, they "seem to eliminate time as a dimension altogether, leaving us with nothing even recognizable as normal

18. See David Papineau, "Tensers" (review of Lee Smolin's *Time Reborn*), *TLS* (Sept. 13, 2013), 23.
19. *Philosophy* (Cambridge University Press, the Royal Institute of Philosophy) 10, no. 39 (July 1935), 380.

change,"[20] thus hopelessly confusing a metaphysical condition with a physical one, without acknowledging the fact. The hypothesis of gravitational waves as an extension of the theory of general relativity proposed by Einstein in 1916 appeared to have found validation exactly a century later, when LIGO detectors situated in Louisiana and Washington both "measured ripples in the fabric of spacetime—gravitational waves."[21] That particular metaphor of rippled fabric is very close to Nabokov's "folding carpet" of time's pliable patterning; indeed, he wrote a short story based on the proposition that waves of gravitation may warp space-time ("Time and Ebb," 1944). In that story undulating Time re-laps and re-lapses upon itself. It is one extended déjà vu in effect, set to illustrate why time "ling'reth in childhood, but in old age fleeteth."

Nabokov's well-known insistence on rereading is a cardinal element of his aesthetics. The principle of rereading entails the notion of reverse reading, that is, going from effect to cause, ultimately from the end to the beginning—of a unit (chapter, part) and of the whole (novel). Rereading also entails, ineluctably, a passive imitation of the author's act of multilayered rewriting of his text. Reading, of course, is nowhere near writing in intensity and sheer compositional ecstasy. There is a quantitative compensation, however: one has reread what the writer wrote many more times than the author did.

Viewed from a different angle, rereading amounts to a spatial reversal of time, a vitally important problem with which Nabokov's deeper-thinking characters (e.g., Van Veen in *Ada* and Vadim Vadimych N. in *Look at the Harlequins!*) grapple

20. Papineau, op. cit., 23.
21. LIGO = Laser Interferometer Gravitational-Wave Observatory. Reported in B. P. Abbott et al., "Observation of Gravitational Waves from a Binary Black Hole Merger," *Physical Review Letters* 116, no. 6 (2016).

so memorably and so futilely. In general, in his Montreux novels, more than in the preceding ones (*The Defense* is the only exception), subsequent readings reveal new layers of previously stored but missed intelligence, discoverable only by sailing back in time, spar-buoy by spar-buoy. The (re) reader of the second half of such a novel is in a regular flood-and-ebb mode, constantly reaching back to earlier chapters for illuminating theme-tracking.[22]

A formal model of backtracking time in prose underpins Nabokov's early English piece with the awkward title "Time and Ebb," where the first word evokes "tide," as in Shakespeare's "the tide of times."[23] Here Time is made, not to warp, as it may in a regular novel, but to boomerang, to fold back onto itself like a tidal wave: Time booming like a tide, ranging like waves. In that story, narrated by a coeval of Nabokov's son Dmitri, the reality of the present time-space (1944, New York City) falls under study by means of an extraordinary application of the making-strange device. Read superficially, it is a wistful account furnished by an astoundingly detailed, clear vision of a beautiful, heroic, imperfect past, recollected from a point of great remove for the benefit of the memoirist's younger contemporaries. But on a higher plane, a pencil of rays is projected into the remote future only to be reflected back onto the world of the story-maker rather than teller, and it is in that strange light that the readers of the *New Yorker*, where the story appeared, were invited to see, as if for the first time, the "brass and glass surfaces" and the "whirr and shimmer of a caged propeller" in the milk bar of a drugstore,

22. In a curious recent case of a "chronic déjà vu" (an interesting choice of adjective), a British man fell into a "constant loop of time": see Emma Ailes, "Terrifying Time Loop: The Man Trapped in Constant Déjà Vu," BBC News, January 24, 2015, www.bbc.com/news/uk-30927102.

23. *Julius Caesar* (3.1.272). Actually, "tide and ebb" would be technically an incorrect antonymy.

or the sunset of a "greenhouse day" in Central Park, with its "old-fashioned . . . lilac-colored . . . aquatic skyscrapers" and "Negro children [sitting] quietly on artificial rocks," or else they, the first readers, were reintroduced to the rum habit of pushing numerous tiny buttons through tight slots in their garments. Time courses back and forth, looping moebiusly as it were, depending on the terrace we take for observation, even though it somehow turns out to be one and the same in the end. Shortly prior to "Time and Ebb," Nabokov tried a peculiar "future in the present imperfect" tense at the very end of *The Gift*, where the hero envisions writing someday the very book that is dwindling in the reader's hands, and also in *The Real Life of Sebastian Knight*, whose surface narrative trick is predicated on moving through the timeflow upstream, from the certain fact of the hero's death to the hazy beginning of his uncertain life reflected in a chronological series of his books. It seems that between 1937 and 1944 Nabokov was trying a complex technique of writing forward whilst narrating backward.

He liked reversals both in word games (he found anagrams and even palindromes irresistible, once writing a perfectly reversible rhymed Russian quatrain into an album of his and Joyce's friend, Lucie Noël Léon, the palindrome of whose maiden-married name could not have escaped Nabokov's eye) and in chess (the so-called retrograde analysis, explained in *Speak, Memory*), and employed both in his writing. *The Gift* and *The Real Life of Sebastian Knight*, the last Russian novel and the first English one, composed adjacently, both employ an elaborate device of real narration running backward, against the current of progressive unfolding of information. The reader of either book learns at the end that there is no end: the storyline begins on the last page and takes you back to the level right above the entrance, in a never-ending helicoid rereading process. Indeed, retrograde analysis may be a happy way to describe Nabokov's axiom of proper reading of a novel. In a chess game, as in life, ground rules forbid taking moves back; but in a retrograde chess problem one is supposed to, indeed must, take moves back, one by one, all the way to the beginning, a solid metaphor for the notion of reading backward, as it were: retracing one's steps. And, to revise Nabokov's favorite dictum, if a book is not worth retracing (checking hidden key points by backing up to the beginning) and rereading (now enlightened by the discoveries made by retrogressing), it is not worth reading the first time.

The principal movement in Nabokov's prose is perhaps that of shuttling, of going back (when memory is at work) and forth (when imagination is engaged), and it is that interaction of memory and imagination that makes true fiction possible and the make-believe powerful, and this is exactly what Nabokov expects the reader to have and to use.[24]

"The future is but the obsolete in reverse," we read in "Lance," Nabokov's last short story,[25] which, unlike "Time and Ebb," is projected plainly into a fathomable future, predicting in reverse, as it were, and thus reversing the etiology of an event. But strictly speaking *"the future is . . ."* is a disagreeable linguistic fallacy, whereby a present-tense verb is made to predicate that which is not in the present. The other grammatical means to express it predicatively in English (and in many other languages) are merely ways to sidestep the conundrum by expressing one's wish or hope or obligation. "Sham Time," Van calls it (perhaps with a nod to *Finnegans Wake*) and further elaborates on that sensible abnegation of the future, that "faculty of prevision."[26]

---

24. The effects of a reverse timeflow can be particularly striking in cinematography, but they are seldom employed to any depth, let alone sophistication. Nabokov might have seen the crude *Escape from the Planet of the Apes* (D. Taylor, 1971), but he would likely find the brilliant shifting of time frames in the television show *Lost* (J. J. Abrams et al., 2004–2010) fascinating.

25. *Stories*, 635.

26. *Ada*, 548, 560.

CLARITY OF VISION

Certain passages . . . sound a prophetic, even doubly prophetic forenote not only of the later atomystique but of still later parodies of the theme—quite a record in its small dark way.

—Foreword to *The Waltz Invention*

Clairvoyance, a term of specifically religious origin and con-notation, does not imply foreseeing the future; rather, it stands for seeing the future as if it were present. "Time and Ebb" stages a somewhat gawky experiment that aims to do just that—but in reverse, since only the actual reader, and not the fictive narrator, knows what is projected, whence, and whither.

With Nabokov, the incidence of a phenomenon for which I cannot find a fitter description than a strangely accurate foreg-limpse of an event that has not yet happened is disconcert-ingly large. Once one has exceeded the number of instances that still feels probable and then sees that number doubled and trebled—rather like in the coin-flipping prologue to Stoppard's *Rosencrantz and Guildenstern Are Dead*—one doesn't quite know what to make of it or what to do with it. It is one of those things that are at once awkward to display and a shame to discard. It is a staggering chance meeting an improbable alternative to chance; their meeting place is aporia.

Those instances range from gratuitous to scientific to mys-tical. On the silly end of it, *Pale Fire*'s narrator's powerful motorcar is called "Kramler," likely a portmanteau of Chrysler and Daimler-Benz. In 1998 the two automakers merged and their official corporate name became "DaimlerChrysler" (they divorced nine years later). In the same novel, Nabokov coins "modem," another happy portmanteau whose currency, since its invention in 1958 until much later, was limited to the US air defense's shorthand for "modulator-demodulator." Nabokov's modems stand for "modern democrats," a funny foresight in hindsight. (This somehow reminds one of Shakespeare's making Hermione exclaim, with restrained pride, "The Emperor of Russia was my father"—more than a century before the first such emperor, Peter I, was proclaimed.)

"I often think," Nabokov once said, that "there should exist a special typographical sign for a smile—some sort of concave mark, a supine round bracket . . ."[27] Now, of course, this ubiquitous smiling roundface grins at you from every screen as a preemptive sign of nonaggression.

Much as he predicted, the late twentieth- and early twenty-first-century "denominations of time" might indeed look to the anglophone people of the earlier twentieth century like "telephone numbers" ("Time and Ebb," 581), as digital clocks in the 1980s supplanted the descriptive half-past-fours in favor of the often excessively precise four-thirty-ones (or even the military-style "sixteen-thirty-one"), then briefly gave room to "analogue" watches while retaining the hyperaccurate time-telling of the digital ones, then yielded the entire what-time-is-it business to electronic devices and, most recently, to computers imitating wrist watches. And while in Antiterra's de-electrified, hydraulic-powered world the "dorophone" (a fantastic telephone stand-in), smart as it may be, does not resemble an iPhone, "the new instantogram" certainly predates the Instagram by half a century.[28]

Here is a more complex case, but just as absurd and as annoyingly "wondrous strange" (to quote Horatio). Following chess moves and names in *The Real Life of Sebastian Knight* takes one on a fascinating journey to a dead end. Even before the book was published, Nabokov told Wilson, who had read it in manuscript and wrote a curious blurb, that ". . . no—except for the sketchy chess-game alluded to in one chapter there is

27. *Strong Opinions*, 133–34.
28. *Ada*, 552.

no 'chess-idea' in the development of the whole book. Sounds attractive, but it is not there."²⁹ A small town called Roquebrune is where Sebastian's mother died. He visits the place, senses her ghostly presence in the pension's garden, only to discover later that she had spent her last months in a different Roquebrune (in the Var rather than Cap-Martin). It seems quite likely that Nabokov chose that particular place because of its faintly chess-sounding name (*roquer* means to castle, i.e., to have a rook leapfrog the king). In 1992, seventy years after Sebastian had sat on that garden bench at Les Violettes, a Dutch tycoon named Joop van Oosterom staged in that very town the first of the twenty annual chess tournaments called "Melody Amber" (after his newly born daughter), with specially invited elite players. That first tournament in Roquebrune, incidentally, was won by a Ukrainian named Ivanchuck.

Here is another curious case of strikingly limpid guess-work verging on augury. Pnin's former wife, Liza Wind, visits him in the piercingly sad second chapter and says:

> "I think I'll lie on your virgin bed, Timofey. And I'll recite you some verses. . . . Listen to my latest poem," she said, her hands now along her sides as she lay perfectly straight on her back, and she sang out rhythmically, in long-drawn, deep-voiced tones . . .

Forty-five years after this was written, Emma Gershtein, a friend of Anna Akhmatova—Liza's paragon in poetry and pose—published her rather scandalous memoir in which one finds this description of an episode in 1941: "Anna Andreevna [Akhmato-va's patronymic] lies in her bed almost all the time, and without even lifting her head from the pillow is reciting for me, muttering as if in trance [*почти бормочет*], her new poem."³⁰

29. *Nabokov–Wilson Letters*, 51.
30. Emma Gershtein, *Memuary*, 264.

In the short story "Double Talk," an atypically topical and therefore somewhat awkwardly stitched together 1945 short story (later renamed "Conversation Piece, 1945"), the narrator encounters a seedy Russian émigré colonel at an implausibly disgusting soirée of German sympathizers. The man is of the kind that Nabokov found particularly repulsive: a "Red Monarchist" and a Soviet end-of-war patriot. The narrator doesn't quite catch his name at introduction: ". . . a Colonel Malikov or Melnikov . . ." Six decades on, a number of display features of the Russian Federation's ideological tenets fit uncannily, almost verbatim, the good colonel's ideals ("The great Russian people has waked up and my country is again a great country. We had three great leaders. We had Ivan, whom his enemies called Terrible, then we had Peter the Great, and now we have Joseph Stalin. . . . Today, in every word that comes out of Russia, I feel the power, I feel the splendor . . ."). Moreover, two prominent trans-Soviet Nabokov critics happen to be called Malikova and Melnikov.

In the fast-moving, toponymical part of *Lolita*, drafted mostly while he himself was traveling across America, Nabokov lists the places where Humbert and Lolita "had rows, minor and major. The biggest ones we had took place: at Lacework Cabins, Virginia; on Park Avenue, Little Rock, near a school . . ." and several more. The Nabokovs passed Little Rock already on their first long-distance motoring in 1941 and might have done it again on a subsequent trip west and southwest.[31] At the beginning of the 1957 school year, that is, at least four years after *Lolita* was finished, nine black students enrolled in the racially segregated Central High School in Little Rock, which caused a crisis that required President Eisenhower's intervention. Central High is on Park Street.

31. See Robert Roper, *Nabokov in America*, 51.

One block down is S. Schiller Street (Lolita was to become Mrs. Schiller).[32]

Among the more absurd osculations of this sort stands out an episode that Nabokov describes in rich detail in one of his interviews, unsuspecting of the punch line. In February 1937, in Paris, he was asked to give a reading on Pushkin as a last-minute substitute for Yolanda Földes, the Hungarian authoress of *La Rue du chat qui pêche*, a pretty ghastly best-selling novel inhabited by faux-Russian farcical characters with names straight from a Hollywood script-book ("'She loves Fedor, not Vassja,' Tuchachevski said to Bardichinov"). As Nabokov entered the Salle Chopin, the Hungarian consul raced to him to express his sympathy, mistaking him for the husband of the suddenly indisposed lady-writer.[33] The husband's name—the name that the good consul had on his lips as he extended his hand to the surprised lecturer—was "M. Clarent," a French homophone of the name of the cemetery where Nabokov was to be buried forty years later.

Nabokov rejected, for serious philosophical reasons, generic science fiction but himself was not alien to the fiction of fore-knowledge, in areas as diverse as geopolitics, psychology, cosmology, and of course his specialized branch of biology. One of Brian Boyd's articles aims to show that Nabokov anticipated certain important recent discoveries about human nature.[34] In "Lance," a fantasy written ten years before the earth could be seen from outer space and a full seventeen years before photographic images of its entire lapis-lazuli globe as it was rising over the moon's horizon were published in Stewart Brand's techno-hippy *Whole Earth Catalog*,

32. The "coincidence" spotted by Jeremiah L. Monk, then a Wesleyan University student.

33. See *Strong Opinions*, 86; Boyd-1991, 434.

34. "Nabokov as Psychologist," in Brian Boyd, *Stalking Nabokov*, 109–22.

Nabokov imagined what it would look like if viewed from another planet:

My young descendant on his first night out, in the imagined silence of an unimaginable world, would have to view the surface features of our globe through the depth of its atmosphere; this would mean dust, scattered reflections, haze, and all kinds of optical pitfalls, so that continents, if they appeared at all through the varying clouds, would slip by in queer disguises, with inexplicable gleams of color and unrecognizable outlines.[35]

Nowadays young descendants look without any excitement at these images, some of which resemble Nabokov's description with astounding accuracy.

A few years ago a shocked scientist published a report in which a DNA analysis proved not only that Nabokov was right in theorizing, at about the time of writing "Time and Ebb,"[36] that certain Blues (butterflies) had come to the New World from Asia but that they came in five distinct waves. "He got every one [of the stages of migration] right," said Dr. Naomi Pierce, curator of lepidoptera at Harvard. "I couldn't get over it—I was blown away," she told the *New York Times*.[37] Moreover, the specific route via the Bering Strait that Nabokov proposed and that seemed improbable at the time (because of the low temperatures) has also received strong support. In *Conclusive Evidence*, he pursues mentally his first butterfly, a captured but escaped Swallowtail, on its forty-year-long flight from Vyra to Vologda to Viatka to Verkhne-Kolymsk (where it lost a tail over the conglomerate of Soviet extermination

35. *Stories*, 639.
36. See his published and unpublished papers and notes of 1943–44, collected in *Nabokov's Butterflies*.
37. Carl Zimmer, "Nonfiction: Nabokov Theory on Butterfly Evolution Is Vindicated," *New York Times*, January 11, 2011.

camps), and from there, across the Bering Strait (how else?), to Alaska, to be at long last recaptured in Colorado.

In a poem composed shortly before "Time and Ebb," Nabokov says that he wants above all to be remembered as a discoverer and describer of a butterfly. But his reputation in the world of biology has now reached much farther, into the elite company of those visionaries who worked at restoration of an unfathomable past, and their vision, though shrugged off as wild by their contemporaries, was pronounced right by a posterity they did not live long enough to catch a glimpse of.

There are several recorded instances of what Nabokov called inklings of his posthumous fame, some light and droll, others strangely factual, all baffling. "I open a newspaper of 2063 and in some article on the books page I find: 'Nobody reads Nabokov or Fulmerford today.' Awful question: Who is this unfortunate Fulmerford?"[38] (This well-known twinkling reply to a silly question has spawned, in half the time predicted, a Fulmerford Club and a webpage that opens on "Yes, I am *that* Fulmerford.") This was a simple projection—a clean 100-year throw from the date of that *Playboy* interview. But here is an earlier and queerer case of a projection reflected. In a 1941 letter to his wife, he whimsically visualizes himself in his present situation from a great temporal distance, much as the narrator of "Time and Ebb" does: ". . . shall I write one *little piece in Russian*—and then translate it? *'While living at Wellesley, amidst oaken groves and sunsets of serene New England, he dreamt of trading his American fountain pen for his own incomparable Russian implement'* (From *Vladimir Sirin and His Time*, Moscow, 2074)."[39] Why that particular year? What was the mnemonic peg here? His 175th anniversary? Why not just pick the round

38. *Strong Opinions*, 34.
39. Cf. *Letters to Véra*, 444.

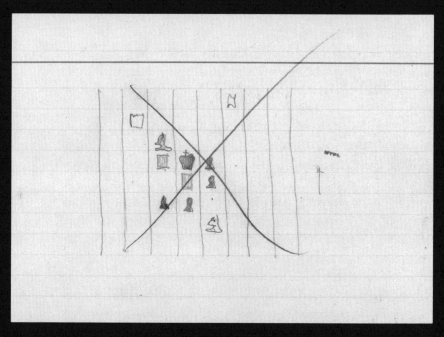

FIGURE 19. An inchoate chess problem, possibly a mate in three, on the verso of the dream card dated November 24, 1964.

bicentenary? In any event, that "and his time" viewed from an untouchable remoteness falls neatly into the theme.

Earlier in this book I dwell on two of Nabokov's prescient dreams, one extraordinarily prodigious, both wondrously Dunnesque.[40] But how would Dunne explain the story of Roman Grynberg's sending Nabokov, in 1957, the first volume of the *Lexicon of Pushkin's Language*, just published in Moscow, in response to which Nabokov wrote back from Ithaca in May of that year: "Dear Roman, thank you for the present and the inscription. You will send me the second volume in 1960, and the last one—in 1977." It was probably nothing but levity: it would take, he implied, the Soviets "forever" to complete the project (in the event, the last volume came out in 1961). However, Nabokov's projected 1977 would be carved in granite on his gravestone twenty years later.[41]

In July 1975 he stumbled and fell ("shot down 150 feet," as he put it in his diary) in the mountains near Davos, almost literally with "a heavenly butterfly in his net, on the top of a wild mountain," to quote from a shiveringly prescient short poem about one plausible setting of his death scene he had composed three years before that fall. It was a recast of Gumilev's famous "You and I," with these lines: "And I shan't die in my bed, a doctor and a notary at my side, but in some remote mountainous crevice choked by wild ivy." In Nabokov's case, the net leapt out of his hand and got caught up in a tree branch, "like Ovid's lyre," and could not be retrieved. Nabokov himself was, eventually; he died in a hospital bed after all, from an apparently unrelated cause. Brian Boyd sees in this episode "Hugh Person stuff,"[42] but Nabokov—supine,

40. See pp. 22–23.

41. R. Iangirov, ed., *Diaspora: Novye materialy* (Paris, St. Petersburg: Athenaeum-Phoenix, 2001), 522.

42. Reference to an episode in *Transparent Things*, Nabokov's next-to-last novel. See Boyd-1991, 652.

upside-down, unable to get up, a cable car quietly floating over him like a spaceship full of gay, waving aliens—might also recall a place from his last novel, just then published, which has a remarkable foreshadowing of an ethereal journey for which this fall could have been a departure point:

> Imagine me, an old gentleman, a distinguished author, gliding rapidly on my back, in the wake of my outstretched dead feet, first through that gap in the granite, then over a pinewood, then along misty water meadows, and then simply between marges of mist, on and on, imagine that sight![43]

Not all of the "Time and Ebb" narrator's recollecting foresights, or, conversely, prognostic remembrances, have come true. The "true nature" of electricity was not discovered "by chance" in the 1970s; the "great flying machines" are still flying, but library index cards have been replaced by intangible catalogs; the great "South American War" has been so far avoided; we still "squeeze . . . buttons into as many buttonholes" and have our "meals at large tables" in a "sitting position," or at least some of us do; and Russia and France not only do not have a common border (a misogermanic Russian's dream) but are now separated also by the Ukraine and the Russian Federation.

In the summer of 1926, a year after their marriage, Véra Nabokov, who was unwell, spent two months at a Schwartzwald resort; Nabokov would write her from Berlin a long letter every night, often with attached self-made word riddles and cryptograms. She wrote back much less often, which led to repeated jocular complaint. In one of his letters he remonstrates that "if we published a little book—a collection of your letters and mine—it would contain no more than

---

43. *Look at the Harlequins!*, 240.

20% of your labours, my love. . . . I suggest that you close the gap—there is still time . . ." The time left was fifty-one years *to the day*: that letter was written on July 2, the date Nabokov was to die. When the collection was published, the "little book" turned out to be an eight-hundred-page three-pounder, in which Véra Nabokov's contribution amounted to zero percent (because she had suppressed and likely destroyed her part of the correspondence). Curiously enough, *Pale Fire* was begun on July 2, 1959, and it is on that day that Gradus is chosen to carry out the regicide. In his copious commentaries to *Eugene Onegin,* Nabokov mentions (as does his creature Pnin in the third chapter of the novel) Pushkin's obsessive *memento mori*, in particular his attempts to preview the "fatidic date" by writing down and then closely examining the digits of various plausibly looking candidate years. Here we seem to see a reversal of sorts: inadvertently assigning mnemonic value to a date that would turn out to be the second date on one's tombstone.

A randomly chosen date for use in fiction; a casually mentioned year in a letter to a friend; a slip of the tongue in a dream on the second day of his experiment; an amusing quid pro quo in a Paris lecture hall—scattered incidentals, trifles if taken singly, yet oddly significant in combination, for they pointed to the time of Nabokov's death and the places of his cremation and burial. He would have admired this design employed in every one of his novels, had he noticed it—that is, had he not been part of it.

Nabokov's looping projections into the future had a secret, if deniable, plane. It is as if he were setting up catastrophic situations in fiction in order to render harmless that very possibility in life. The belief that life resists predictability is nothing new, of course, but essaying it in one's art, so as to preempt an untoward turn in life, is not common. Here again,

Nabokov certainly knew the precedent of Pushkin, two of whose 1829 poems had to do with this sort of inoculative divination: "Whether I roam . . . ," with its memorable lines ". . . Where am I destined to expire—in combat, travels, or in waves?"[44] and "Traveller's Complaints" (1829)—a long list of more or less improbable manners of death on the road (e.g., by being whacked on the head by a swing-beam a clumsy operator might drop at a crossroads).

His prophylactic explorations of more plausible disasters had much more to do with his wife and son than with himself. In a sequel to *The Gift*, Godunov-Cherdyntsev's wife dies in a car accident; the differently widowed Sineusov, in the unfinished novel *Solus Rex*, madly wants to believe that his dead wife's spirit may be able to communicate; his desperate idea is to try to reverse time and effect a restoration in an imaginary setting of a novel, but even in fiction within fiction she meets with a violent end all the same.[45] The theme of some terrible danger threatening a son or a daughter—invariably only one and often of an age close to Nabokov's only son Dmitri at the time of writing—runs through his early novels and stories written in America. David Krug (*Bend Sinister*) is tortured to death by the brutal socialist-collectivist tyranny; Dolores Haze (*Lolita*) is kidnapped by a talented monomaniac; Lancelot Bok ("Lance") is about to leave behind, for the second and apparently last time, his elderly, stoically adoring parents, to explore the perilous depths of space. In *Pnin*, his only noncatastrophic (in the classical sense of the term) novel, the richly gifted Victor Wind is lucky to be spared the harm that his addle-headed, Freud-befuddled parents were to inflict on him, just as his "real" father Pnin narrowly escapes the

44. Nabokov quotes these verses in *Pnin* (ch. 3) and in the short story "Cloud, Castle, Lake" (1937).

45. See Nabokov's preface to the English version: *Stories*, 680.

snares of his uncharitable narrator. In 1942 Nabokov wrote a little projection poem of the forfending-by-forestalling type, published only once and never collected:

When he was small, when he would fall,
on sand or carpet he would lie
quite flat and still until he knew
what he would do: get up or cry.

After the battle, flat and still
upon a hillside now he lies—
but there is nothing to decide,
for he can neither cry nor rise.[46]

And in the shortest and saddest of his English short stories, the postwar "Signs and Symbols," Nabokov makes the nameless elderly couple dread that their only son, a teenager beset by an apparently congenital mental illness very much akin to autism, might have succeeded after several thwarted suicide attempts. The ending of that story is open like a trapdoor, inviting equally to enter and to avoid. Before the end, the mother is going through old pictures in the family album: "Four years old, in a park: moodily, shyly, with puckered forehead, looking away from an eager squirrel as he would from any stranger." The park, we learn, was in Leipzig where the family lived at the time. In June 1936 Nabokov's wife and son spent a month in Leipzig, and in one of his letters to her from Berlin, he responded to something in her previous: "Strange he's afraid of squirrels."[47] Without the later short story this would perhaps be unremarkable. But it is even more striking for the fact that this passage could be based on Véra Nabokov's sketches of Dmitri's childhood that Nabokov had urged her to write and on which chapter 15 of his memoirs (about their son) relies:

46. *Atlantic Monthly*, January 1943, 116.
47. *Stories*, 600–601. *Letters to Véra*, 274.

Once, I remember, he was desperately frightened. It was on his first trip (to Leipzig) and his first walk in the city park dedicated to the preservation of wildlife—as much of it as there could be preserved in a fairly large city. Pigeons, common and huge ringdoves (were they ringdoves?), squirrels, ducks, all of them so tame that they walked around your feet in circles waiting for crumbs, and innumerable small birds, grown so cheeky that they constantly try to peck at your sandwich between the lunch basket and your mouth. And an occasional rabbit or two playing in the middle of some vast lawn (not quite so tame—they would scurry for cover when you came nearer). This sudden exposure to nature had an unexpected result. A baby who loved to run around (and a fast runner he was) suddenly became a little lap-baby. He refused to take a step. He refused to be carried by familiar and friendly people (aunt, uncle), but clung to me in despair yelling when I tried to put him down for a minute (a big baby, a heavy armful of a baby).[48]

CONCLUSION

The real writer should ignore all readers but one, that of the future, who in his turn is merely the author reflected in time.

—The Gift[49]

Any fiction must harness time and reproduce its progress. At higher levels this illusion is made to resemble time-elapsing by techniques similar to cinematic montage: synchronization,

---

48. "Véra Nabokov on Dmitri's Childhood," undated, autographed typescript (6 pp.), Manuscript Box: "Nabokov, Vladimir Vl., Biographical and Genealogical Notes," Vladimir Nabokov Archive, Berg Collection, New York Public Library. I am grateful to Professor Olga Voronina for pointing out this source.
49. Second imaginary dialogue.

juxtaposition, jump-cutting, etc. Nabokov perfected the art of time management in a novel by flipping the hourglass, as it were, so that events which had not yet happened could be checked against those that had, reversing the chain of causality.

The butterfly chapter in *Conclusive Evidence* ends on a singular pronouncement without an elaboration: "I confess I do not believe in time." The Russian version, which is generally smoother, softer-lit, and sadder, is less terse and more lyrical in this instance as well: "I confess I do not believe in transient time [*mimoletnost' vremeni*]—a light, gliding, Persian time!" That last attribute, Persian, makes for a smooth transition to his favorite carpet-folding metaphor for Time folding onto itself, making the past present. Yet, in a sense, the dry English statement suffices, for not believing in time is tantamount to not accepting degradation of such nonperishables as love, soul, and mimetic art. If the clarifying synonym of time is change, then "transient time" is a redundancy.

The last chapter of that memoir opens on a homophonic twisting of Horace's line: "They are passing, posthaste, posthaste, the gliding years." Horace was calling out, plaintively, repeatedly, his friend's name: "Postume, Postume"; Nabokov, in the very next sentence, makes clear that not only this last chapter but the entire book is done in the same vocative case—is addressed to "you," to his friend and wife. Time that seemed to stand still now is slipping by in midstream, rushing toward the end of a book whose secret purpose was to dam timeflow and make it go back. That name, Postumus, which initially meant "born late," went on to mean "posthumous."

Nabokov's grave in the Swiss Clarens has the plain *écrivain* under his name and next to the dates that stake off the distance of time between the "two abysses," prenatal and

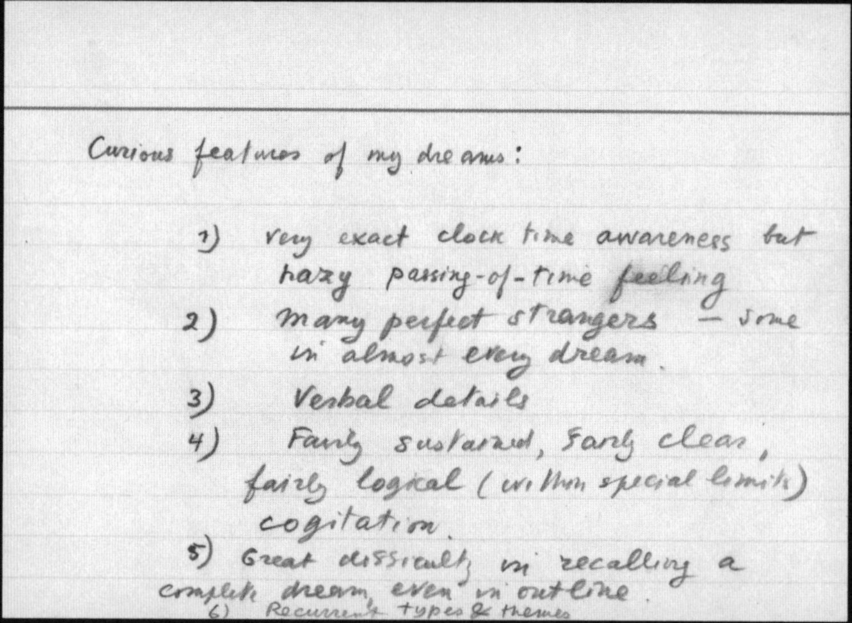

Curious features of my dreams:

1) very exact clock time awareness but hazy passing-of-time feeling
2) Many perfect strangers — some in almost every dream.
3) Verbal details
4) Fairly sustained, fairly clear, fairly logical (within special limits) cogitation.
5) Great difficulty in recalling a complete dream, even in outline.
6) Recurrent types & themes

FIGURE 20. This card, "Curious features of my dreams," appears among the dream records of November 1964.

postmortal. The plain restraint of that single word shorn of modifiers is designed to carry the weight of significance. But no matter the significance, it only scratches the surface (which is the literal meaning of the word "writer" in Germanic, Romance, and Hellenic languages) of what the wordsmith really does. Like no other verbal artist before him, Nabokov shaped his observations, sensations, suppositions, and conclusions in supremely exquisite compositions, all the time experiencing, and experimenting with, that "draught from the past." Toward the end of his life he lets out a sigh in an unpublished Russian poem: if only he were given a dozen more years to live (*"prozhit' eshcho khot' desiat' let"*), to sense a "draught from Paradise" (*"skvozbiak iz raia"*).[50] It was as if Nabokov felt an invisible presence of a time vortex, where the warm wind of the past meets the much lighter and cooler current of the foretold but unpredictable future, blowing "between remembrances and hope—that memory of things to come."[51] In an earlier Russian poem about the wind from the past the poet foresees his future reader feeling that same wind touching his forehead. Meteorologists call it a reversal wind, *vent de retour*. In a later English poem about the rain "travelling into the past," the poet, looking rearward, hopes against hope that the evershining beginning of life is secure from later inclemencies:

How mobile is the bed on these
nights of gesticulating trees
when the rain clatters fast,
the tin-toy rain with dapper hoof
trotting upon an endless roof,
travelling into the past.

50. Written on an index card, in a folder now in a private archive in Palm Beach, Florida.
51. From "Dom" (Home), a 1919 poem by Khodasevich that Nabokov certainly knew: «между воспоминаньемъ и надеждой, / сей памятью о будущемъ».

Upon old roads the steeds of rain
slip and slow down and speed again
through many a tangled year;
but they can never reach the last
dip at the bottom of the past
because the sun is there.[52]

There is yet another important Russian sentence absent in
Speak, Memory. The last passage of chapter 6 begins: "I have
wandered far—yet my past is still by my side, and a particle
of the future is also with me."

Speaking of particles: in 2011 the Hadron Collider, the
world's largest subatomic particle accelerator situated on
the opposite shore of the lake where Nabokov composed
Transparent Things some forty years earlier, beamed a jet of
neutrinos, those ghostliest of particles that penetrate any
material density, from point A in Geneva to point B in Gran
Sasso in Italy, some 684 versts away (which happens to be
the perfectly exact distance between the Moscow Fair Square
and the Senate Square in St. Petersburg). Much to the bewil-
derment of the scientists, it exceeded the speed of light, out-
stripping it by an astonishing sixty feet.[53] The speed of light
limit is the bedrock of Einstein's theory: all modern physics
and, by extension, much of modern philosophy depend on
it, including the origin of the universe and its conjurable age.
At speed exceeding that of light, an object so traveling is,
according to one bemused physicist, "lighter than nothing,
has negative width, and time goes backwards."[54]

52. "Rain," in *Poems* (1959).

53. A retest done by a different team, reported on March 15, 2012, did not confirm
the initial finding (see arXiv.org/abs.1203.3433) but, in a sort of accelerated Poppe-
rian cycle, immediately generated calls for a re-retest.

54. See Michio Kaku's report in the *Wall Street Journal*, September 26, 2011. Much
of this was proposed in detail about ninety years earlier by Florensky in his book
Mnimosti v geometrii [Imaginary Values in Geometry] (Moscow: Pomorie, 1922) and
developed by Alexey Losev.

Lurking among the draft notes for "A Detail of the Ornament," a technical tour-de-force short story Nabokov published as "The Circle" (1934), there is a neatly compact sentence, unrelated to the story, which offers a surprising and original, if indirect, explanation of why he wrote fiction and even why he wrote it the way he did:

> How can I not cosset, cherish, adorn my earthly life, which in the Kingdom to come will serve me as an enchanting amusement, a precious toy for my immortal soul.[55]

Cossetting, cherishing, and adorning life in an imaginary reconstruction of its givenness accessible (1) to the senses, (2) to psychological empathy, and (3) to metaphysical intuition was Nabokov's lifelong artistic self-assignment. His incessant efforts aimed to probe, by artistic means, the riddle of human existence between the oblivion of what he calls the "infinite foretime" in *Pale Fire* and that toward which one is heading. That quest led him to peer into the mystery of death and afterlife, and so it is natural that Nabokov's fiction can be viewed as a string of exploratory tests of various possibilities, from an almost Orthodox tenet formulated by Dandilio in *The Tragedy of Mr. Morn* (1924, the year of Van's essay on Time), to the extraordinary attempt at self-erasure in what is left of his last, unfinished novel.

When, in 1944, Nabokov made the nonagenarian narrator of "Time and Ebb" write, circa 2020, that he "can discern the features of every month in 1944 and 1945 but seasons are utterly blurred when I pick out 1997 or 2012," he seems to describe nothing more than the well-known foreshortening of an aging memory. He could not, of course, foresee

---

55. "Какъ мнѣ не нѣжить, не пѣстовать, не украшать моей земной жизни которая въ царствѣ будущаго вѣка будетъ служить прелестной забавой, дорогою игрушкой для моей безсмертной души." The Berg Collection, New York Public Library. Folder in Manuscript Box: *Detal' ornamenta.*

that his son, who was of the same age as the story's narrator, would die in 2012 on reaching precisely the terminal age of his father. And yet, in the peculiar system of Nabokov's late-life beliefs, from these seemingly arbitrary coincidences a gentle fogwind blows coming from the unknowable, forever arrested present tense of the story's author, in the reversible perspective of space without dimension, and time without duration.

PERMISSIONS
ACKNOWLEDGMENTS

NABOKOV WORKS CITED

MANUSCRIPT SOURCES

*The Henry W. and Albert A. Berg Collection of English and
American Literature at the New York Public Library*

Records of dreams in the 1964 experiment: Manuscript Box "Notes for work in progress"
Excerpts from diaries: Manuscript Box "Diaries 1943–1973"
A note for an unidentified, unfinished prose: Manuscript Box *Detal' ornamenta*
An excerpt from Véra Nabokov's memoir: Manuscript Box "Biographical and Genealogical Notes"

The Private Electronic Archive of Dmitri Nabokov

Transcript of the 1964 dream records (imperfect but used as reference when the original presented difficulty)

PUBLISHED WORKS CITED IN THIS BOOK

Ada, or Ardor: A Family Chronicle. New York: McGraw-Hill, 1969. Reprint, New York: Vintage, 1990. Page references are to the first edition.
Bend Sinister. New York: Time/Life Books, 1964. Reprint, New York: Vintage, 1990. First published 1947. Page references are to the 1964 edition.
Camera Obscura. Ann Arbor, MI: Ardis, 1978.
The Defense. New York: Vintage, 1990.
Despair. New York: Paragon Books, 1979. Reprint, New York: Vintage, 1989. First published 1966. Page references are to the 1979 edition.
The Eye. New York: Phaedra, 1965. Reprint, New York: Vintage, 1990. Page references are to the 1965 edition.
The Gift. New York: Putnam's Sons, 1963. Reprint, New York: Vintage, 1991. Page references are to the 1963 edition.
Glory. New York: McGraw-Hill, 1971. Reprint, New York: Vintage, 1991. Page references are to the first edition.

Invitation to a Beheading. New York: G. P. Putnam's Sons, 1959. Reprint, New York: Vintage, 1989. Page references are to the first edition.

King, Queen, Knave. New York: McGraw-Hill, 1968. Reprint, New York: Vintage, 1989. Page references are to the first edition.

Laughter in the Dark. New York: New Directions, 1960. Reprint, New York: Vintage, 1989. First published 1938. Page references are to the 1960 edition.

Letters to Véra. Edited by Brian Boyd and Olga Voronina. New York: Knopf, 2015.

Lolita. In *Nabokov: Novels 1955–1962*. New York: The Library of America, 1996.

Look at the Harlequins! London: Weidenfeld and Nicolson, 1974. Reprint, New York: Vintage, 1990. Page references are to the 1974 edition.

Mary. New York: McGraw-Hill, 1970. Reprint, New York: Vintage, 1989. Page references are to the first edition.

The Nabokov–Wilson Letters, 1940–1971. Ed. Simon Karlinsky. New York: Harper & Row, 1979.

The Original of Laura. New York: Knopf, 2009.

Pale Fire. In *Nabokov: Novels 1955–1962*. New York: The Library of America, 1996.

Pnin. In *Nabokov: Novels 1955–1962*. New York: The Library of America, 1996.

Poems. Garden City, NY: Doubleday, 1959.

The Real Life of Sebastian Knight. New York: New Directions, 1959. First published 1941. Page references are to the 1959 edition.

Speak, Memory. In *Nabokov: Novels and Memoirs, 1941–1951*. New York: The Library of America, 1996.

The Stories of Vladimir Nabokov (abbreviated as *Stories*). New York: Vintage International, 2008.

Strong Opinions. New York: McGraw-Hill, 1973.

The Tragedy of Mr. Morn. Translated by Anastasia Tolstoy and Thomas Karshan. London: Penguin, 2012.

Transparent Things. New York: McGraw-Hill, 1972. Reprint, New York: Vintage, 1989. Page references are to the first edition.

SELECT BIBLIOGRAPHY

Alexandrov, Vladimir. *Nabokov's Otherworld.* Princeton, NJ: Princeton University Press, 1993.

Aserinsky, E., and N. Kleitman. "Regularly Occurring Periods of Eye Motility and Concomitant Phenomena, during Sleep." *Science* 118 (3062) (September 1953): 273–74.

Barabtarlo, Gennady. *Aerial View: Essays on Nabokov's Art and Metaphysics.* New York: Peter Lang, 1993.

———. "Nabokov's Trinity: On the Movement of a Nabokov Theme." In *Nabokov and His Fiction.* Ed. Julian Connolly. 2nd ed. Cambridge: Cambridge University Press, 2012.

———. *Sochinenie Nabokova* [Nabokov's Composition]. St. Petersburg: Limbach, 2011.

Bergson, Henri. *Duration and Simultaneity: Bergson and the Einsteinian Universe.* Ed. Robin Durie. Manchester: Clinamen Press, 1999.

———. *Matter and Memory.* London: Dover, 2004.

Blackwell, Stephen. *The Quill and the Scalpel: Nabokov's Art and the World of Science.* Columbus: Ohio State University Press, 2009.

Borges, Jorge Luis. *Selected Non-Fictions.* Ed. Eliot Weinberger. New York: Viking, 1999.

Boyd, Brian. *Stalking Nabokov.* New York: Columbia University Press, 2011.

———. *Vladimir Nabokov: The American Years.* Princeton, NJ: Princeton University Press, 1991.

———. *Vladimir Nabokov: The Russian Years.* Princeton, NJ: Princeton University Press, 1990.

Boyd, Brian, and Robert Michael Pyle, eds. *Nabokov's Butterflies.* Boston: Beacon Press, 2000.

De la Mare, Walter. *Behold, This Dreamer!* New York: Alfred A. Knopf, 1939.

Dement, W., and N. Kleitman. "The Relation of Eye Movements during Sleep to Dream Activity." *Journal of Experimental Psychology* 53 (5) (1957): 89–97.

Dunne, J. W. *An Experiment with Time.* 4th ed. London: Faber & Faber, 1944.

Einstein, Albert. *Relativity: The Special and General Theory.* Trans. Robert W. Lawson. New York: Pi Press, 2005.

Florensky, Pavel. *Beyond Vision. Essays on the Perception of Art.* Ed. Nicoletta Misler. Trans. Wendy Salmond. London: Reaktion Books, 2002. Abbreviated as Florensky-2002.

Florensky, Pavel. *Iconostasis*. Trans. D. Sheehan and Olga Andrejev. Crestwood, NY: SVS, 1996.

———. *Sochinenia v chetyrekh tomakh* [Collected Works in Four Volumes]. Moscow: Mysl'. Vol. 2, 1996 (=Florensky-1996); vol. 3 (1), 1999 (=Florensky-1999); vol. [7], 2000 (=Florensky-2000).

Garfield, Simon. *Timekeepers: How the World Became Obsessed with Time*. Edinburgh: Canongate, 2016.

Gershtein, Emma. *Memuary*. St. Petersburg: Inapress, 1998.

Gleick, James. *Time Travel: A History*. New York: Pantheon, 2016.

Hildebrandt, F. W. *Der Traum und seine Verwertung für Leben*. Leipzig, 1875.

Jolas, Eugene. *Man from Babel*. New Haven, CT: Yale University Press, 1998.

Levy, Eric P. *Detaining Time*. New York: Bloomsbury, 2016.

Maury, Alfred. *Le sommeil et les rêves*. Paris, 1878.

McCarthy, Cormac. *The Crossing*. New York: Alfred A. Knopf, 1994.

Michotte, Albert. *The Perception of Causality*. London: Methuen, 1963.

Miyake, A., and P. Shah, eds. *Models of Working Memory*. Cambridge: Cambridge University Press, 1999.

Pitzer, Andrea. *The Secret History of Vladimir Nabokov*. New York: Pegasus, 2013.

Roper, Robert. *Nabokov in America: On the Road to Lolita*. New York: Bloomsbury, 2015.

Schiff, Stacy. *Véra (Mrs. Vladimir Nabokov)*. New York: Random House, 1999.

Schredl, M., D. Atanasova, K. Hörmann, J. T. Maurer, T. Hummel, and B. A. Stuck. "Information Processing during Sleep: The Effect of Olfactory Stimuli on Dream Content and Dream Emotions." *Journal of Sleep Research* 18 (3) (2009): 285–90.

Smolin, Lee. *Time Reborn*. Boston: Houghton Mifflin Harcourt, 2013.

Tammi, Pekka. *Problems of Nabokov's Poetics*. Helsinki: Suomal. Tiedakatemia, 1985.

Unger, Roberto, and Lee Smolin. *The Singular Universe and the Reality of Time: A Proposal in Natural Philosophy*. Cambridge: Cambridge University Press, 2014.

Wood, Michael. *The Magician's Doubts: Nabokov and the Risks of Fiction*. London: Chatto & Windus, 1994.

Wulff, Oskar. "Die umgekehrte Perspektive und die starke Niedersicht." In *Kunstwissenschaftliche Beiträge*. Leipzig, 1907. 1–40.

Zimmer, Dieter E. "What Happened to Sergey Nabokov?" January 2, 2017. http://dezimmer.net.

Zunzhine, Lisa. *Why We Read Fiction: Theory of Mind and the Novel*. Columbus: Ohio State University Press, 2006.

NAME INDEX

Akhmatova, Anna, 175
Aldanov, Mark, 27

Bentley, Edmund C., 91n98
Berberov, Nina, 88, 88n89, 92
Bergson, Henri, 6
Borges, Jorge L., 7n
Boyd, Brian, 175, 179
Bromberg, Elena, 87
Burgess, Anthony, 96

Callier, Jacqueline, 82, 82n73
Chaykovski, Petr, 82
Chklaver, Georges, 88, 88n90
Clark, Petula, 87, 87n85
Cross, Samuel H., 5n

Dante Alighieri, 166
De la Mare, Walter , 6, 16
Dobuzhinski, Mstislav, 68, 68n56
Dostoevski, Fyodor, 39n
Dunne, John W., 14–15, 19–23, 33n2, 34, 37, 37n8, 46, 47n17, 56, 95, 115, 119, 134, 163, 167–68; his dreams, 10–12, 23; his experiment, 12–13, 20, 86, 89; his life, 4–7; his theory, 7–10

Einstein, Albert, 6, 15, 169, 190
Eliot, T. S., 6

Fairbanks, Gordon H. , 5n
Fasolt, Sophia (VN's cousin), 85, 85n81

Feigin, Anna, 23, 24n, 70n58, 87, 96–97
Flaubert, Gustave (*Madame Bovary*), 99, 99n10
Florensky, Priest Pavel, 14–18, 78, 97n3, 165, 165n12, 190n54
Földes, Yolanda, 177
Fondaminsky, Ilia, 26, 26n25, 108
Freud, Sigmund, 6, 15, 18nn16 and 17, 19–21

Gershtein, Emma, 175
Gregory, Joshua, 168
Grynberg, Roman, 5n, 181
Gumilev, Nikolay, 181

Heidegger, Martin, 6
Hessen, George, 104, 104n13
Hinton, C. H., 6
Hitler, Adolf, 39
Hofeld, Evgenia K., 98, 98n7
Horace, 187
Huxley, Aldous, 6

Jolas, Eugene, 6n
Joyce, James, 6, 160, 166

Kalashnikov, Mikhail, 48 and 48n
Karpovich, Mikhail, 87, 87n86, 99
Karpovich, Tatiana, 87, 87n86
Kerenski, Alexander, 102, 102n
Khodasevich, Viacheslav, 26 and 26n26, 27, 108, 189n51
Korff, Baroness Maria von, 98
Kubrick, Stanley, 26

Ledkovski, Marina, 86n82
Léon Noël, Lucie, 171
Losev, Alexey, 190n54

Mandelstam, Osip, 68n57
Markevich, Topazia, 65, 65n44
Mason, A.E.W., 37n8
Massalsky, Princess Elena, 84, 84n78
McCarthy, Cormac, 163
McTaggart, J. M., 168
Monk, Jeremiah, 177n32
Mostel, Samuel, 90, 90n95

Nabokov, Dmitri (VN's son), 3n3, 40,
    40n10, 57, 79, 85, 170, 184–86, 192;
    in VN's dreams, 44–46, 55, 64–65,
    67 ("perhaps"), 70, 76, 80–81, 87,
    92 ("vaguely"), 105, 108
Nabokov, Elena (mother), 52; in VN's
    dreams, 53, 57, 59–62, 77; 97n4
Nabokov, Kirill (brother), 91, 91n96
Nabokov, Sergey (brother), 27, 53
Nabokov, Véra (wife), 3n3, 30, 35n4,
    42, 105; 37, 41, 63, 74, 82, 90–91,
    108 ("I love you"), 182–83, 184, 187
    ("you"); her dreams, reported, 44–45,
    46–47, 52, 57 ("irretrievable"), 64,
    65, 73, 74, 76, 84, 86–87; her memoir
    sketch, 185–86; in VN's dreams, 35,
    39, 46, 48, 49–50, 62, 64, 65–66, 70,
    80, 81, 85, 87, 88, 92, 96–97, 99, 105;
    in VN's "fatidic" visions, 68, 86; in
    VN's letters, 107
Nabokov, V. D. (father), 82, 98, 119;
    refracted in VN's fictional dreams,
    25, 151–56; in VN's dreams, 2,
    61–62, 76–77, 81, 99, 102, 105–6
Nikolay Andreevich (cook), 81, 81n71

Papineau, David, 168n18, 169n20
Paulhan, Jean, 71, 71n61

Pierce, Naomi, 178
Pelé, Edson Arantes, 107
Petkevich, Olga (sister), 87, 87n87
Planck, Max, 6
Priestly, J. B., 6
Proust, Marcel, 160
Pushkin, Alexander, 183–84

Rausch von Traubenberg, Baron
    George (cousin), 56–57, 57n31
Rolf, Filippa, 76, 76n66
Rukavishnikov, Vasily (uncle), 25–26
Russell, Bertrand, 168

Selivonik, Tatiana, 86n82
Shakespeare, William, 170,
    170n23, 174
Sikorski, Elena (sister), 24n, 27, 63,
    63n42, 73, 76
Sikorski, Nilly , 62n40, 63
Sikorski, Vladimir (nephew), 62–63,
    62n40, 80, 89
Shifrin, Semyon, 92n99
Slonim, Sophia, 52
Solntsev, Konstantin, 97n4
Stoppard, Sir Tom, 173

Tolstoy, Count Leo, 87, 160
Turgenev, Ivan, 2, 99, 99n11

Ustinov, Peter, 74, 74n, 80
Ustinov, Suzanne, 74, 74n, 80

Voronina, Olga, 186n48

Wells, H. G., 6
Wilson, Edmund, 3n6, 85, 85n79, 119,
    174–75

Zak, Alexander, 106, 106n15
Zimmer, Dieter, 164n9

INDEX OF NABOKOV TITLES